A WARREN BENNIS BOOK
This collection of books is devoted exclusively to new and exemplary contributions to management thought and practice. The books in this series are addressed to thoughtful leaders, executives, and managers of all organizations who are struggling with and committed to responsible change. My hope and goal is to spark new intellectual capital by sharing ideas positioned at an angle to conventional thought—in short, to publish books that disturb the present in the service of a better future.

Books in the Warren Bennis Signature Series

Branden,
Self-Esteem at Work

Mitroff/Denton,
A Spiritual Audit of Corporate America

Schein,
The Corporate Culture Survival Guide

Sample,
The Contrarian's Guide to Leadership

Lawrence/Nohria,
Driven

Cloke/Goldsmith,
The End of Management and the Rise of Organizational Democracy

Cleveland,
Nobody in Charge

Previous Books by Harlan Cleveland

Next Step in Asia (1949), with John K. Fairbank, Edwin O. Reischauer, and William L. Holland

The Overseas Americans (1960), with Gerard J. Mangone and John Clarke Adams

The Obligations of Power (1966)

NATO: The Transatlantic Bargain (1970)

The Future Executive: A Guide for Tomorrow's Managers (1972)

China Diary (1976)

The Third Try at World Order: U.S. Policy for an Interdependent World (1977)

Humangrowth: An Essay on Growth, Values, and the Quality of Life (1978), with Thomas W. Wilson Jr.

The Knowledge Executive: Leadership in an Information Society (1985)

The Global Commons: Policy for the Planet (1990), with papers by Murray Gell-Mann and Shirley Hufstedler

Birth of a New World: An Open Moment for International Leadership (1993)

Leadership and the Information Revolution (1997)

Edited by Harlan Cleveland

The Art of Overseasmanship (1957), with Gerard J. Mangone

The Promise of World Tensions (1961)

The Ethic of Power: The Interplay of Religion, Philosophy and Politics (1962), with Harold D. Lasswell

Ethics and Bigness: Scientific, Academic, Religious, Political and Military (1962), with Harold D. Lasswell

Energy Futures of Developing Countries: The Neglected Victims of the Energy Crisis (1980)

Bioresources for Development: The Renewable Way of Life (1980), with Alexander King and G. Streatfeild

The Management of Sustainable Growth (1981)

Prospects for Peacemaking: A Citizen's Guide to Safer Nuclear Strategy (1986), with Lincoln P. Bloomfield

Nobody in Charge

Essays on the
Future of Leadership

Harlan Cleveland

Foreword by Warren Bennis

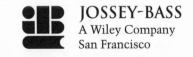

JOSSEY-BASS
A Wiley Company
San Francisco

Published by

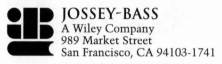

JOSSEY-BASS
A Wiley Company
989 Market Street
San Francisco, CA 94103-1741

www.josseybass.com

Copyright © 2002 by Harlan Cleveland.

Jossey-Bass is a registered trademark of John Wiley & Sons, Inc.

The adaptation of Chapter 2 is used with permission from World Business Academy. The adaptation of Chapter 3 is reprinted from *Futures*, Volume 31, Harlan Cleveland, "The Global Century," pp. 887–895. Copyright © 1999, with permission from Elsevier Science. The adaptations of Chapters 6 and 9 are used with permission from the World Future Society, 7910 Woodmont Avenue, Suite 450, Bethesda, MD 20814.

Jossey-Bass books and products are available through most bookstores. To contact Jossey-Bass directly, call (888) 378-2537, fax to (800) 605-2665, or visit our website at www.josseybass.com.

Substantial discounts on bulk quantities of Jossey-Bass books are available to corporations, professional associations, and other organizations. For details and discount information, contact the special sales department at Jossey-Bass.

We at Jossey-Bass strive to use the most environmentally sensitive paper stocks available to us. Our publications are printed on acid-free recycled stock whenever possible, and our paper always meets or exceeds minimum GPO and EPA requirements.

Library of Congress Cataloging-in-Publication Data

Cleveland, Harlan.
Nobody in charge: essays on the future of leadership / by Harlan Cleveland; foreword by Warren Bennis.—1st ed.
p. cm.—(The Warren Bennis signature series)
Includes bibliographical references and index.
ISBN 0-7879-6153-1 (alk. paper)
1. Leadership. I. Title. II. Series.
HD57.7 .C56 2002
303.3'4—dc21   2002001908

FIRST EDITION
HB Printing   10 9 8 7 6 5 4 3 2 1

Contents

For Lois

Foreword:
The Man on the Flying Trapeze

When the Jossey-Bass editors and I first began dreaming about starting a new series, we agreed on One Big Thing: that we were going to seek out the most imaginative works that were at an angle to conventional thought, to publish books that would disturb the present in the service of a better future.

I can't think offhand of a book that incarnates that dream we had in mind as does this prescient and elegantly written book. It is a unique contribution, one that I'm confident will be read, "hi-lited," and dog-eared by future generations of reflective practitioners and just about anybody else interested in the leadership of human organizations and their fate.

In his informal autobiography I happened to get my hands on some time ago, Harlan Cleveland wrote:

> Just before Christmas 1960, Dean Rusk [Secretary of State] called to ask me to take on the multilateral diplomacy bureau in State and coordinate the actions taken by U.S. representatives in most of the fifty-three international organizations to which the United States then belonged. I figured (correctly as things turned out) that in the web of U.S. tensions on U.N. policy I would be "the man on the flying trapeze"—trying to figure how to coordinate, from below, a trio of strong players: Adlai

Stevenson in New York, Dean Rusk in the State Department, and President Kennedy in the White House. Apprehensive about the potential risks yet relishing the coming complexities, I drew a deep breath and said yes.

Harlan has been saying yes to complexity and challenge his entire life, and what is most interesting about him and what gives this remarkable book the rich texture is the hinterland of his experience. He has been at the elbow of history since the 1930's (when he was in his very early twenties) and every decade since then. He was in Europe in 1939 (at Oxford, as a Rhodes Scholar) when World War II broke out; a civilian warrior at age twenty-three with the Board of Economic Warfare in Washington, helping pick out industrial targets for the Air Force to bomb; in Italy in 1944 starting to put Italy back together again; then in China after the war to manage the U.N.'s huge relief program (UNRRA); then back in Washington helping manage the Marshall Plan for European recovery.

It seemed at times that he was not only an observing participant but a perceptive observer and player in the major world events of the last half of the 20th century. He was executive editor of what was probably the best magazine of politics in the 1950's, *The Reporter*. In the 1960's, he was an Assistant Secretary of State, then was tapped to be Ambassador to NATO. He also had three leadership posts in higher education—President of the University of Hawaii and dean of two distinguished graduate schools: of public administration (the Maxwell School at Syracuse) and public affairs (the University of Minnesota's Humphrey Institute, of which he was founding dean in the 1980's).

I won't mention all of Harlan's achievements, except that on top of his day jobs, he always managed to write some of the best essays and books on public and private leadership. While I always thought that I had one or two prophet rods in my one book bag, Harlan was always ahead of the curve, mine or anyone else's. I wouldn't be surprised to learn that he invented the curve. I'll mention only three of his classics, always worth another read: *The Future Executive*, *The Knowledge Executive*, and *Birth of a New World*.

Those book titles show the range and knowledge of this philosopher/well, not king, but certainly, prince. Harlan Cleveland has not only made history; he wrote it. The titles also reveal Harlan's unique range of interests. Along with very few others, such as James MacGregor Burns and Barbara Kellerman, he yoked together the theory and practice of public leadership with the work of those who have written about leadership in the private sector.

In this book, *Nobody in Charge*, Harlan weaves a fascinating tapestry of how the New World of knowledge and information will influence the context and ecology and leadership of contemporary organizations.

This is a wise book, an elegant book, a book that illuminates the darkness of complexity, chaos, and uncertainty by a man who knows not only how to navigate that trapeze but to thrive, and have fun, while doing it.

Santa Monica, California   Warren Bennis
February 2002

Preface

When Warren Bennis and I first started talking (by e-mail) about collecting some of my writings on leadership in a book of essays, I was arguing mostly with myself. I had no doubt that it would be fun to reread and massage a few of my many writings. Yet I wondered whether there was a market for essays if the author's name doesn't happen to be Ralph Waldo Emerson.

The certain joy of rediscovery soon triumphed over the market uncertainty—which is anyhow more for the publisher than for an author to weigh. All my life I have been a compulsive writer around the edges of fulltime work. Since my work was, for nearly half a century, some variety of executive leadership, I was always tempted to mine my own experience for insights on leadership—which I have defined, in action and in writing, as *bringing people together to make something different happen*.

The theme that brings these fifteen essays together in one volume may need a moment—but only a moment—of explanation. There are four simple steps in my argument: Step 1: Nobody's in charge. Therefore (Step 2) everybody has a chance to be partly in charge. But (Step 3) most people will not, for one reason or another, reach for that brass ring. Consequently (Step 4) those who do will find that they are "leaders."

No one is a leader in everything; we're all followers in most things. But wherever each of us decides to take a lead—by pointing the way, or forming an organization, or whatever—the "how" of leadership has obviously been mutating rapidly, and requires attitudes and skills very different from what worked in past centuries, or even in most of the twentieth century.

In raking over my old coals I have been delighted to find so many that are still warm—and some that are even hotter now, measured by public and professional interest, than when they were written. This is partly because I got interested early in what the accelerated spread of knowledge, enhanced by the marriage of computers with global telecommunications, would mean for leadership.

While speculating—in a variety of jobs in and out of government—on what the "Information Revolution" would mean for education, for fairness, for business, for governance, for diplomacy, and for world affairs, I naturally kept trying to decipher its message for the changing roles of leaders in private or public enterprise, in America and around the world.

Because I have always set more store by what I see happening than what I read might happen, I thought I owed the reader at least a sketch of what I was doing during the twentieth century— to give you a better sense of my angle of vision, and why I got interested so early and so often in leadership. An informal autobio, in a narrative form no résumé adviser would approve, comes right after this Preface.

Since this book isn't a mystery story, it starts with two essays that try to sum up the new environment for the exercise of leadership, and a third that suggests why the worldwide spread of information is fundamentally changing what it takes to bring people together to make things happen.

The macrotransition we are in is illustrated by the leadership role of people who are still called *followers* (Chapter Four). It has changed the dynamics—who leads whom, and how—within the big organizations so characteristic of modern society; they look top-heavy but have to diffuse authority and initiative broadly in order to work at all (Chapter Five).

The same transition, powered by the spread of knowledge, is visible in international affairs: nobody is, or can be, in charge of the world. But the United States is "the fat boy in the canoe," as Dean Rusk (Secretary of State from 1961 to 1969) used to say. So, in trying to help make the world "safe for diversity," Americans are learning new styles of leadership in world affairs (Chapter Six). The organized brainwork of science and technology needs to be matched by the brainwork of leaders about how to point scientific discovery toward human needs and purposes, and how to tame the technologies that follow from discovery (Chapter Seven). The macrotransition so complicates everything that leaders need to hone their nonrational intuition, ponder the patterns and probabilities of chaos, and come to think of complexity as fun (Chapter Eight.)

The second half of the book focuses on the attitudes, qualities, and learnings that I believe will work best for people who lead in the changing knowledge environment of the twenty-first century. While I was leading on the hoof, I kept trying to reflect on and write down what I was learning. Some of those reflections were first drafted even before I started (in the seventies) looking at leadership through the many-colored prism of the knowledge revolution. That they made the cut into this book just means that in the year 2001, with a good deal of updating and rewriting to be sure, I think they have survived the constantly changing test of relevance.

The last three essays focus on the ethical stance and whole-system philosophy of the "situation-as-a-whole person," and on the implications for education of citizens when a rapidly growing proportion of our citizenry will be taking the lead in one context or another.

The first Afterword sums up some of the recurring themes you'll find discussed in more depth in the essays; this short piece was originally written for *The New York Times* as a comment on diplomacy, one of many modes of leadership. The other Afterword is a brief comment on the leader as generalist, made when I accepted a Swiss international prize for "accomplished generalists."

———

To characterize with a single phrase the multifaceted global transformation in which we are all now finding our way is daunting for a writer—and likely to be awkward for the reader. It certainly has much to do with the marriage of computers and communications, which I long ago started calling "the great social event of the 1980s." The pallid phrase "Information Revolution" did help us get our minds around the revolutionary impact of the fusion of ever-faster computers with increasingly reliable telecommunications.

But "Information Revolution" fails to describe or connote the dramatic spread of knowledge as individuals by the hundreds of millions use the power of organized information to broaden and deepen their own thinking, and reinforce their insistence on participating in decisions affecting their own destiny. Nor does it highlight the way intuition and spiritual insight, partly based on rational thought but sparkling well beyond it, are needed to achieve wisdom—which each of us needs to guide the human choices we make, to decide what to *do* from day to day.

Trying to express in one word this whole complexity of mind and spirit, I have chosen *knowledge* as the inclusive word to use in phrases such as "the spread of knowledge," "the knowledge society," and "the knowledge environment." I know that individual thinking, let alone group and collective thinking, is much more complicated than the reason-bound word *knowledge* as defined in our dictionaries. But until our common language reflects how complex reality is, it will have to do.

———

In dipping into these essays, you may want to know that for more than a half a century I have carried—first in my wallet, then engraved on my memory, an admirably succinct and now-familiar nugget of wisdom from Lao-tzu (who wrote in the sixth century B.C.), certainly one of history's very wisest commentators on leadership:

> Of a good leader, who talks little,
> When his work is done, his task fulfilled,
> They will all say, "We did this ourselves."

Falcons Landing   Harlan Cleveland
Sterling, Virginia
February 2002

How I Got Here
(An informal autobio
by Harlan Cleveland)

Since my work experience has been rather varied I am often asked, by students and others, what my favorite job was. I have responded, with complete honesty, that it was what I was doing at the time. Maybe this is because I never planned my life, or selected a career, or tried to figure out what a next job would lead to. I just decided as I went along that I would tackle the most interesting and difficult task that presented itself, preferably something that I didn't have a clear idea how to do—because I would learn more that way.

The Thirties

My long life fits rather neatly into decades. During the 1930s, in my teens, I was naturally in school—for three years in France and Switzerland, then Andover ('34), then Princeton ('38), then one year (1938–39) at Oxford as a Rhodes Scholar—until Hitler marched into Poland and changed my life, along with other lives by the hundreds of millions.

During those formative prewar years, I had focused my studies on politics, government, and international affairs. The big noise in America was President Franklin D. Roosevelt's New Deal. So late in 1939 I drifted to Washington, D.C., where I got off to a lively professional start as an "intern" in government and also found a lifelong love life with another intern, Lois Burton from Salem, Oregon. We were married in Washington, in the sweltering summer of 1941, and we're still happily together; our sixtieth wedding anniversary came up in July 2001.

The Forties

My internship (with Senator "Young Bob" LaFollette of Wisconsin) and a first government job in the Farm Security Administration (as a writer, not a farmer) were exciting and congenial, but another life-changing event, the Japanese attack on Pearl Harbor in December 1941, made me a sudden economic warrior at age twenty-three. In the Board of Economic Warfare, a vigorous young civilian with a yen to "bring people together to make something different happen" seemed to be much in demand, so I was catapulted early into executive jobs.

A childhood accident had irreparably damaged my right eye. The local draft board kept drafting me, but in the medical screenings the eye-doctors kept saying no. By 1944, when the draft board finally said I could go abroad as a civilian, I was a specialist on the Italian economy, first helping to pick industrial targets for the Air Force to bomb, then helping plan the reoccupation of Sicily and Southern Italy, as the Allied forces attacked the "soft underbelly" of Hitler's Europe.

So my natural next step (as a civilian in uniform, with no rank, which meant any rank) was to join the Allied Control Commission (ACC) in Rome, where at age twenty-six I became executive director of its Economic Section, supervising (or so it said on the pyramidal organization chart) a staff of fourteen hundred people, mostly military officers including American colonels and British brigadiers. We tried, successfully, to help get a new democratic Italian government started so the Allies could, as Roosevelt and Churchill had agreed, "give Italy back to the Italians."

With the war in Europe won, the United States and Britain moved fast to make the United Nations Relief and Rehabilitation Administration (the largest U.N. operation ever) responsible for restoring the Italian economy. Late in 1945 I became deputy chief of mission of a suddenly enlarged UNRRA operation; we brought into Italian ports "three ships a day" of food, fuel, farm equipment, and industrial tools that provided the start-up for Italy's postwar economic miracle.

By the spring of 1947, UNRRA was closing its European operations but decided to continue for one more year its largest country program, a massive infusion (worth $650,000,000 in 1947 dollars) of relief and rehabilitation supplies into China. UNRRA's biggest project anywhere was the earth-moving equivalent of building the Panama Canal: rebuilding hundreds of miles of dikes to bring the great silty Yellow River, which had been wandering all over North China during World War II, back into its old riverbed. UNRRA's China Office, headquartered in Shanghai, included fifteen regional offices, operations on both sides of the civil-war battle lines, and altogether four thousand staff members.

The director of that office was a genial and effective American, Major General Glen Edgerton of the U.S. Army Corps of Engineers, a former governor of the Panama Canal. Early in 1947 he became ill and had to come home, and I was plucked out of Italy on a few weeks' notice to take his place. By then I was (a rapidly maturing) twenty-nine; I think I learned more in that one year in China, about large-scale management and about cross-cultural sensitivities, than in any other five years of my life.

In 1948, with UNRRA phasing out and the Chinese Communists winning the civil war, I returned to Washington just as the Marshall Plan for European Recovery was going through Congress. Congress tacked onto the Marshall Plan legislation a sizable program of aid to "China"—meaning the Nationalist government of Chiang Kai-shek. Since I was just back from China, I looked like an expert. When Paul Hoffman came to Washington to head the new Economic Cooperation Administration (ECA), he quickly asked me to handle China aid—and keep it from distracting the much larger European effort.

By the autumn of 1949, the People's Republic of China had con-
quered the Chinese mainland, and the "China" for which our aid was
destined was limited to the island of Taiwan. The United States then
decided to use part of the China aid money to set up aid programs in
"the general area of China." I was put in charge of a Far Eastern Program that included a crescent of countries, from South Korea and Taiwan through the Philippines around to Indonesia and Burma—and
also Vietnam, Laos, and Cambodia, which would, a short generation
later, play so large and divisive a role in American history.

The Fifties

By 1950 I had become part of ECA's central management, and in
1952 was appointed assistant director for Europe in the new Mutual
Security Agency, responsible for supervising from Washington—
and defending on Capitol Hill—the fourth and final year of the
Marshall Plan. General Dwight D. Eisenhower was elected that fall
to succeed Harry S Truman as president. Although my payroll category was still in the civil service, my responsibilities in the Truman
administration would surely make me look to the incoming Repub-
licans like a political appointee; I reckoned it was a good moment
to explore the private sector.

A friend from my Italian period, Max Ascoli, had started a new
national magazine, *The Reporter*, in New York City. Early in 1953 I
took him up on his standing invitation to join him, first as executive editor and later also as publisher. This provided me, as the magazine company's executive vice president, with a sudden opportunity
for intensive learning about U.S. business enterprise. It was admittedly a somewhat distorted learning, since I was surveying the landscape for successful small businesses whose profits could offset our
magazine's hefty losses. By replicating the Kaiser-Willys merger, in
which heavy loser Kaiser had bought the profitable manufacturer of
the Jeep, we managed in time to create a breakeven Reporter Mag-

azine Company: one loss-leader plus three small but profitable communication firms.

In the fall of 1956, I took another leap into the unknown. The Maxwell Graduate School of Citizenship and Public Affairs at Syracuse University, then (and now) the nation's premier school of public administration, was losing its dean, and wanted to appoint as his successor a "reflective practitioner" with hands-on experience in government. The outgoing dean, Paul Appleby, and I were both speaking at a political science conference in Philadelphia; he sidled over after my talk and said, "How would you like to succeed me?" Just like that. I liked the idea very much. But this was a prominent academic deanship; I had never even taught in a university, and World War II had aborted my doctorate at Oxford. The faculty had to swallow hard, but swallow they did, so in my first university job I became both a dean and a full professor with tenure. That's the way to start an academic career.

At Syracuse, I found that the Maxwell School dean not only presided over the high-profile Master's degree in public administration. I was also the dean of all the social science departments, their graduate work and also their undergraduate offerings. So my introduction to academic administration was both broad and deep. For almost five years (1956–1961) in that job, I also managed a Carnegie study of Americans abroad; that led to my first hardcover book—*The Overseas Americans* (McGraw-Hill, 1960)—written with two colleagues on the Maxwell faculty.

The Sixties

While working in New York City and living in suburban Larchmont, I had had a fling at running for a town council in heavily Republican Westchester County. That cured me of elective politics. But I was much attracted to *policy* politics, and in New York State an upstate Democrat was then a rare enough species to have plenty of opportunities. I hosted Senator John F. Kennedy when he visited Syracuse in 1958 to give the Commencement address, served as a Kennedy delegate to the 1960 Democratic National Convention in Los Angeles, and chaired the Citizens for Kennedy campaign in Central New York.

With Kennedy's election, my logical next step was back to Washington. Among the options was one that mightily intrigued me: Assistant Secretary of State for International Organization Affairs struck me as a delightfully complicated place to be, in a world where more and more substantive policy was made in multilateral forums. It became even more interesting when Adlai Stevenson, a world figure who had twice run for president, decided to accept the post as U.S. ambassador to the United Nations, and urged that I become his "backstop" in Washington.

Dean Rusk, a good friend who had tried to persuade me to join him when he was president of the Rockefeller Foundation, also was eager for me to join the new administration. (The announcement that Rusk would be President Kennedy's Secretary of State happened to coincide, one Sunday, with an article of mine titled "Memo to the Next Secretary of State," published in the *New York Times Magazine*.) Just before Christmas 1960, Dean Rusk called to ask me to take on the multilateral diplomacy bureau in State and coordinate the actions taken by U.S. representatives in most of the fifty-three international organizations to which the United States then belonged. I figured (correctly, as things worked out) that in the web of U.S. tensions on U.N. policy, I would be "the man on the flying trapeze"—trying to coordinate, from below, a trio of strong players: Adlai Stevenson in New York, Dean Rusk in the State Department, and President Kennedy in the White House. Apprehensive about the potential risks yet relishing the coming complexities, I drew a deep breath and said yes.

I will leave to my memoirs the many fascinating stories of almost five years in that job. These encompassed not only the front-page dramas (such as the Bay of Pigs and the Cuba Missile Crisis) in which the U.N. played a role. They also involved the handling of global issues (some of the early peacekeeping operations, the World Weather Watch, smallpox eradication, the Outer Space treaties, the Law of the Sea, civil aviation, and arrangements to divvy up the electromagnetic frequency spectrum) which, mostly ignored by the media, were equally fascinating parts of the job.

After President Kennedy was assassinated in 1963, the new president, Lyndon B. Johnson, also very strong in very different ways, asked most of the Kennedy appointees to carry on. Reelected in 1964, he made some changes, one of which was to send me to Paris in 1965 as U.S. ambassador to the North Atlantic Treaty Organization (NATO). There, I had two proximate bosses, Secretary of State Dean Rusk and the Secretary of Defense, Robert S. McNamara. I found myself in the midst of complexities compounded: French objections that led to a wholesale move of NATO from France to Belgium; innovations in nuclear planning (secrecy had been a virus, more openness among the allies was the cure); the decision to launch a NATO communications satellite; the chronic Cyprus issue, threatening war between two NATO allies, Greece and Turkey; the reach beyond planning for war to planning how peace could be made with the Soviet Union; and the U.S. war in Vietnam, which became a deafening offstage noise for the Atlantic Alliance.

I was held over at my NATO post for a few months (January-May 1969) by the incoming Nixon Administration. During that time, some friends in Hawaii who knew I would need a next job arranged an invitation. It seemed almost unfair: Lois and I were invited, toward the end of winter, to leave the shrouded skies of Brussels and spend a week, expenses paid, in sunny Honolulu, to discuss whether to become the next president of the University of Hawaii. There were other options: to my surprise, the new Secretary of State, William Rogers, asked me to go to Rome as Ambassador to Italy. But I was very curious about the turbulence on American campuses in the sixties and anxious to try a university presidency, which looked like the ultimate in complexity management. So, after a summer spent writing a book about the Atlantic Alliance (*NATO: The Transatlantic Bargain*, Harper & Row, 1970), Lois and I moved to Honolulu in the fall of 1969.

The Seventies

The Hawaii adventure started with a year of crisis management. Resentment of the war in Vietnam was at fever pitch, and the university's big main campus was the scene of frequent demonstrations. The president's office was the nearest symbol of authority, so I did a thriving educational business my first year, leading impromptu seminars on the barricades. I also finished, during that initial year in Hawaii, my first book on leadership, *The Future Executive* (Harper & Row, 1972).

But the balanced growth of the nine-campus University of Hawaii was my main preoccupation. We developed the community colleges (in Hawaii, they are part of the state university) as instruments of a real "open admissions" policy; started a law school and a medical school; developed the world's best site for terrestrial astronomy on top of Mauna Kea, an extinct volcano; and expanded both the marine sciences and Asian studies. The weather was wonderful; we enjoyed the active support of a visionary governor, John Burns; the ethnic mix of the population made for a distinctive politics in which "everybody's a minority"; and the university was an enormous factor in every aspect of Hawaii's life: my last year there, one out of every sixteen residents of the state was a student in its university system. Then the steeply rising curve of university revenues suddenly flattened out as a recession hit the islands.

The Aspen Institute was deciding just then to become a much more international think tank, and I joined it in 1974 to develop and direct its new Program in International Affairs based in Princeton, New Jersey. This provided an opportunity for much thinking and many published writings, and for bringing experts from around the country and around the world to summer sessions at Aspen, Colorado—on arms control policy, on issues of growth policy, on global fairness (in a project called The Planetary Bargain), and on international human rights. For me, it was an exciting opportunity for leadership in "thought leading to action."

The Eighties

In 1980, yet another chance to build something new presented itself. The University of Minnesota had decided to build a major new school of public affairs, and make it the living memorial to Hubert H. Humphrey, the popular longtime U.S. Senator who had been vice president of the United States and had run for president in 1968. I became the founding dean of the new Hubert H. Humphrey Institute of Public Affairs, and had a chance to put into practice much of what I had learned both about public affairs and about academic administration. Minnesota, which produces more than its share of lively and imaginative leaders, turned out to be an ideal community in which to invent new modes of leadership education.

During the seventies I had become fascinated with the speedy and pervasive growth of computers and how their fusion with new communications technologies would probably change the future of everything. My continuing study of these trends, and my effort to guess their impact on organizational forms and leadership styles, led to a book published in 1985, *The Knowledge Executive* (Dutton).

In parallel with the institution building in Minnesota, I joined with several colleagues in convening a worldwide group of reflective practitioners and practice-minded scholars to "rethink international governance." On the assumption that, sooner or later, an end to the cold war would require fundamentally new kinds of international cooperation, we called this an experiment in "postwar planning without having the war first." One outcome of this project was a book titled *Birth of a New World* (Jossey-Bass, 1993).

The Nineties

From 1991 to 2000, I served as president of the World Academy of Art and Science, a nonofficial network of not more than five hundred individual Fellows from diverse cultures, nationalities, and intellectual disciplines, "chosen for eminence in art, the natural and social sciences, and the humanities." Its activities focus on "the social consequences and policy implications of knowledge." As a genuine network, with no full-time staff anywhere, the World Academy's center of initiative is inherently the president's office. I took the obligation seriously, and learned a good deal about leading by electronic mail and computer-based teleconferencing.

Since 1988 I have been officially retired, in the sense that I've been living mostly on pensions that pay me for what I *used* to do. But an assortment of board memberships, lecture dates, and writing projects keep converting my retirement into something like a full-time job, based in an office-in-home (harlancleve@cs.com).

Nobody in Charge

Part I

The Macrotransition We Are In

Commentary on Chapter One

The notion of the leader as generalist is a hardy perennial in my writings. But modern societies give such high marks for specialized excellence that the highest degrees awarded by our universities are for deep research in the narrowest fields of expertise. To many people, therefore, the word *generalist* still connotes sloppy or superficial thinking, unthinking or uninformed action.

Chester Barnard, a corporate CEO who became a public official in the state of New Jersey, provided in *The Functions of the Executive* (1938) one of the earliest systematic theories about leadership in the modern era. Yet even he made fun of his own trouble in describing it. "When I have been asked: 'What do you do?' I have been unable to reply intelligibly." A leader, he argued, often takes ideas about what to do and how to lead from the very people he leads: "This sometimes gives the impression that he is a rather stupid fellow . . . and a filcher of ideas. In a measure this is correct. He has to be stupid enough to listen a great deal. . . . If he used only his own ideas he would be like . . . a one-man orchestra, rather than a good conductor, who is a very high type of leader."

The intuition and instinct to "connect the dots," to understand "the intervals between the notes," to focus on the interconnections among specialties and disciplines, to stir experts together to serve a general purpose, is not awarded higher education's highest degree for a good reason: these have to be learned mostly by doing. The art of getting it all together is, well, an art.

1

The Get-It-All-Together Profession

Paradox of Participation

There was a time, celebrated in song and story, when leadership was entrusted to people called *leaders*. Their numbers were tiny, their information scarce, their expertise primitive, the range of their options narrow, the reach of their power marginal, the scale of their actions limited. But they were at least presumed to be "in charge."

In those days it was possible to believe that policy was actually made by people others called *policymakers*. The policymaking few made broad decisions, it was said (and even taught in schools). A much larger group of unsung experts, civil servants, and employees converted these principles into practices. The obligation of most people was to comply with the regulations, pay the taxes and prices established by the few, and acquiesce in the seizure of power by divine right, coup d'état, corporate takeover, or elections sometimes bought or stolen.

In Aristotle's Athens, Confucius's China, Cicero's Rome, Charlemagne's Europe, and Jefferson's Virginia, the educated and affluent few did the social planning and made the destiny decisions that made the difference between war and peace, poverty and prosperity, individual freedom and collective coercion, minority rights and majority rule. The mostly uneducated "lower orders" of slaves, servants, peasants, workers, and merchants—and most women—

were not expected and did not expect to join in the elegant conversations about policy. In those vertical, pyramidal societies, dogma, doctrine, and dictation were the natural style of leadership.

Somewhere along the way in the colorful story of people getting things done, the collection of processes we now call modernization made the vertical society obsolete. Man-as-manager had to learn how to manage the complexity that man-as-scientist-and-engineer and man-as-educator were making both possible and necessary. In a world of intercontinental conflict, gigantic cities, congested living, and large and fragile systems of all kinds, the traditional modes of leadership, featuring "recommendations up, orders down," simply did not work very well. Nobody could be fully in charge of anything, and the horizontal society was born.

The key to the management of complexity was the division of labor. The benefits of modernization were available only to societies that educated most of their people to function as specialists in a division-of-labor economy. Thus there came to pass, late in the second millennium A.D., slaveless societies that responded to a technological imperative by giving citizenship to all their people and legislating education as an entitlement for all their citizens. Thomas Jefferson foresaw this macrotrend as early as 1813. "An insurrection has . . . begun," he wrote to John Adams, "of science, talents, and courage, against rank and birth, which have fallen into contempt." He was spending his postpresidential years building the University of Virginia and promoting education and scholarship from his Monticello home.

When every man, and now every woman too, is entitled to earn through education an admission ticket to active citizenship, when leadership is not the province of a few hundred noblemen, a few thousand big landholders and shareholders, but is shared among an aristocracy of achievement numbering in the millions, decision making is done not by a club but by a crowd. So the core issue of executive leadership is a paradox of participation: *How do you get everybody in on the act and still get some action?*

Leading by Doing

If the get-it-all-together people used to be born to rank and wealth, now they are mostly made—and self-made—by competition and competence. This is true not only in the United States. Today, in all but a rapidly dwindling number of still-traditional societies, men and women become leaders by what they *do*.

Even among authoritarian regimes, the nations still governed by extended families (Saudi Arabia, and some of the Emirates in the Persian Gulf) are greatly outnumbered by those ruled by self-appointed tyrants who got where they are by elbowing their way to power (often by coup d'état), and usually to personal prosperity as well. The closest thing to a ruling class is to be found these days in totalitarian regimes; in each of them, a small group of people who have fought their way up the bureaucratic ladder maneuver for power and preferment and, when they get to the top, achieve only a precarious lifetime tenure—sometimes shortened by sudden death.

In the United States and the other industrial democracies in the Atlantic Community and the Pacific Basin, the aristocracy of achievement is now growing in size and pervasive in function. These people are usually leaders because they want to be—often assisted, selected, promoted, or adopted as protégés by earlier achievers. (None of us, of course, can lead in everything we touch; all of us are followers in most of our life and work.)

People may be leaders in public or private employ, but that distinction is increasingly indistinct in our mixed economy. They may be leaders in politics or business or agriculture or labor or law or education or scientific research or journalism or religion or community issues; some swing from branch to branch in the forest of occupations; some specialize in advocacy or lobbying on policy issues ranging from abortion rights to the municipal zoo. They may be in the establishment or in the antiestablishment. Their writ, conferred or chosen, may run to community affairs, to national decisions or global issues, to a whole multinational industry or to a narrower but deeper slice of life and work: a single firm, a local agency, a neighborhood.

I have tried several times to count the number of leaders in the United States of America. In the mid-1950s, because I was publisher of a magazine I wanted them to buy, I counted 555,000 "opinion leaders." A 1971 extrapolation of that figure came out at about a million. Seven out of ten of these were executive leaders of many kinds of organizations; this "aristocracy of achievement" was estimated in 1985 at one out of every two hundred Americans. After that I gave up: the knowledge revolution keeps multiplying the numbers of Americans who take the opportunity to lead, at one time or another, on one issue or another, in one community or another.

The galloping rate of growth of complexity means that a growth curve of the requirement for leaders (if anyone were clever enough to construct such an index) would show a steeper climb than any other growth rate in our political economy.

Attitudes of Leadership

Every person who seeks or assumes a leadership role in an information-rich society has to develop some of the aptitudes and attitudes of the generalist. Generalists have to be skeptical of inherited assumptions—because so many of them are being undermined so fast by the informatization of society.

They have to be curious about science-based technology—because those who would control it must first understand, not how it works, but what it can do for us and to us. (That's the way most of us understand an automobile: we can't fix it, but we're good at driving it.) They have to be broad in their perspective—to take account of the disappearing distinctions between public and private and between domestic and foreign. They have to be eager to pull people and ideas together—rather than split them apart. They have to be really interested in issues of fairness—because the people to be pulled together are. And they have to be self-confident enough to work, not out of sight in a back room, but riskily out on a limb in an increasingly open society.

You will find in these essays more emphasis on attitudes than on skills. Attitudes are the hardest part of the generalist's required learning. Survival and growth in the get-it-all-together profession, perhaps the world's most difficult line of work, requires a mindset that is, by and large, neglected in our education.

I first tried to define this mindset many years ago before a convention of city managers, because I thought they do some of the world's toughest and least rewarded work. After that I kept trying out on executive audiences and student seminars a series of draft formulations until I thought I had it about right.

Just then a book called *The One Minute Manager* hit the bestseller lists. So I tried to compress in a similar compass, for an op-ed article titled "The One Minute Leader," the generalist mindset I had been drafting and redrafting. My tongue was only half in cheek. There had to be a market niche for a learning tool that leaders, who are usually in a hurry, could absorb on the run.

Those of us who presume to take the lead in a democracy, where nobody is even supposed to be in charge, seem to need an arsenal of eight attitudes (reading time: one minute) indispensable to the management of complexity:

- First, a lively intellectual curiosity, an interest in everything—because everything really is related to everything else, and therefore to what you're trying to do, whatever it is.

- Second, a genuine interest in what other people think, and why they think that way—which means you have to be at peace with yourself for a start.

- Third, a feeling of special responsibility for envisioning a future that's different from a straight-line projection of the present. Trends are not destiny.

- Fourth, a hunch that most risks are there not to be avoided but to be taken.

- Fifth, a mindset that crises are normal, tensions can be promising, and complexity is fun.

- Sixth, a realization that paranoia and self-pity are reserved for people who *don't* want to be leaders.

- Seventh, a sense of *personal* responsibility for the *general* outcome of your efforts.

- Eighth, a quality I call "unwarranted optimism"—the conviction that there must be some more upbeat outcome than would result from adding up all the available expert advice.

No Generalist Ladder

Generalists may start as scientists or MBAs or lawyers or union organizers or civil servants or artists, or mobilizers of feminist or ethnic groups, or citizen-advocates of a particular cause. They may be managers who (as a committee of the International City Management Association put it) know how to "lead while being led." They may even be judges who know that the law has to be molded to reflect both technological change and public opinion. There is actually no generalist ladder to leadership. Every young person starts as a specialist in something; but a rapidly growing minority of them, by accident or motivation or both, graduate into generalist leadership.

They are, with exceptions to be sure, men and women who are not preoccupied with formal power or position, or with getting their faces on TV or their names in the newspapers, people whose concern exceeds their confusion and may even preempt their egos, because they get busy and inventive doing something that hasn't been done before—and have fun doing it. But what makes them the shock troops of the get-it-all-together profession is, above all, their overriding concern for the *general* outcome of their efforts.

Some practicing generalists are legislators and editorial writers and other situation-as-a-whole people whose administrative responsibilities are comparatively light. But most of them are not only leaders but executives in business, government, or the independent sector—that is, people who feel the need not only to point the way to the future, but also to try to get there.

We who practice as executive leaders come in all sizes and shapes, pursue a wide variety of goals and purposes, and operate in many modes—in federal, state, and local bureaus, in big corporations, in small businesses, in academic settings, in nonprofit agencies ranging from the EXXON Education Foundation to Alcoholics Anonymous. But we are all responsible, for our own behavior and decisions, to people-in-general.

The buck doesn't stop with any of those intermediate bodies from which we derive our mandates: legislatures, stockholders, boards of directors or trustees. What Harry Truman said of the U.S. presidency is true for each of us who presumes to bring people together to make something different happen: "The buck stops here."

The Road to Leadership

If you now regard yourself as a leader or have aspirations in that direction, I can with some confidence trace your double career.

First you pick a specialty: legal services or health care, engineering or economics, accounting or architecture, production management or consumer advocacy, weaving or welding, brainwork or manual skill or some combination of the two. As you rise in your chosen field (we used to say "rise like cream in a milk bottle," but homogenized milk in an opaque carton has spiked that metaphor), you find yourself drawn into broader supervisory, managerial assignments, and then into the generalist role, either in your own right or (more likely at first) as staff assistant to a leader whose preoccupation with the whole you are expected to share.

You may be (to adapt some of John Gardner's words) a clarifier, definer, critic, or teacher. Or you may be an implementer, manager, problem solver who will "redesign existing institutions or invent new ones, create coalitions and fight off the people who don't want the problem solved." Or again, you may be counted among the "mobilizers" who "catalyze the social morale, help people know what they can be at their best, and nurture a workable level of unity." You may even come to be effective in all three roles; a good many people are.

This broader role requires a capacity for integrative thinking you didn't learn in school, "people skills" that were not graded and scored earlier in life, attitudes that differ in fundamental ways from those that made you a rising young specialist. Graduating from successful specialist to generalist leader is a wrenching, demanding, sometimes traumatic change of life.

As you shift gears, you will already have had a good deal of practice getting around in, and getting around, large-scale bureaucracies: foiling the personnel classification system, outwitting the budgeteers, hoodwinking the organization analysts, suffering the auditors, and even getting some better furniture for your office. You will also have learned, if you are considered a promising "comer," that despite those pyramidal organization charts the real world of work consists mostly of horizontal relationships. Most of the people you see from day to day don't work for you, and you don't work for them. You work together, even if that isn't the way it looks on the chart.

You will thus already have explored in action the leadership of equals, and tried to get things done in consensual systems—learning, for example, that overt confrontation is more likely to produce resistance than results. This environment will also have required you to cultivate the suasive arts, to learn the constructive uses of ambiguity, to develop the self-restraint not to cross bridges until you come to them, and to practice such conventions of committee work as introducing your personal views by attributing them to others. ("What I hear you all saying is. . . .")

The geometry and gimmickry of bureaucratic behavior are some-times taught as "business management" or "public administration," or even as "advanced management." They are, indeed, essential sur-vival skills in societies full of public and private bureaucracies. The bird that never learns to get around in its environment—that is, to fly—will never go far.

But the critical dimension of leadership, and the centerpiece of education for leadership, is not the technology of office work and committee sitting. That's the easy part. The hard part is organizing your mind for the analysis and projection of breadth.

Breadth: "The Intervals Between the Notes"

Breadth is a quality of mind, the capacity to relate disparate facts to coherent theory, to fashion tactics that are part of a strategy, to act today in ways that are consistent with a studied view of the future.

No one person can know enough to send a team of people to the Moon, in the sense that grandpa and grandma could know everything important about managing their corner grocery store. (The best of the old grocers virtually kept the inventory in their heads, as many merchants in Mideastern bazaars, West African "mammy-wagons," and Oriental jewel markets still do today. But imagine trying to keep in your head the list of spare parts for the space shuttle.) So different kinds of people, with very different kinds of knowledge and skills and personalities and personal goals and networks of friends and acquain-tances, have to be brought together in organizations designed to trans-mute their separate expertnesses and their collective insights into wise day-to-day decisions in the service of a shared objective, *together*.

Breadth is not a contradiction of depth, but its complement. Everything really is related to everything else: the person who plumbs the depths of any specialty finds more and more connections with every other specialty. The astronomers who reach far back in time to postulate a big bang must in scholarly honesty ask the humanistic next questions: *Why* the bang? Who set it off? What does it *mean?* And so the experts come, by the circuitous route of pure reason, to speculations that can only be explorations of faith.

The Scientific Revolution, and its younger siblings the Industrial Revolution and the Information Revolution, were made possible by our capacity to divide into separate disciplines the proven methods of inquiry, and to retrieve from bins of manageable size and complication the knowledge we accumulated by observing, experimenting, and theorizing. But in the latter part of the twentieth century, we came to realize that most of our troubles stem from neglecting the interconnections of knowledge, the interdisciplinary character of all real-world problems. (Chaos theory, discussed in Chapter Eight, seems to have been developed by brilliant oddballs who delighted in breaching disciplinary frontiers.)

Isaac Stern, who was not only a superb musician but a philosopher of music education, was once asked in a public forum at the Aspen Institute why all professional musicians seemed to be able to play the same notes in the same order, yet some sounded wonderful and others did not. The world's best violinist paused and scratched his head. "But it isn't the *notes* that are important," he objected. "It's the intervals *between* the notes." A wise comment, not only about music but about other forms of knowledge. It's not mainly our capacity to dig out "the facts," but rather the educated reason and practiced intuition to relate them to each other and arrange them in meaningful patterns that make the human brain something more than a data-collecting machine with a computerized memory.

Just the same, executive leaders are very likely to be unsuccessful unless they have, earlier in life, put in some time as first-rate specialists. It really doesn't matter in what field. In the offbeat words of poet Charles Olson:

> Best thing to do is *to dig one thing or place or man* until you yourself know more about that than is possible to any other

man. It doesn't matter whether it's Barbed Wire or Pem-
mican or Paterson or Iowa. But exhaust it. Saturate it. Beat
it. And then U KNOW everything else very fast: One sat-
uration job (it might take 14 years), and you're in, forever.

You don't leave behind the attitudes that served you so well when
your primary task was to get to the bottom of whatever-it-was. The
get-it-all-together person needs above all to be good at judging
whether the experts who stream through the executive office, creating a chronic condition of information entropy on the executive's
desk, are getting to the bottom of their subjects. An executive who
has never had personal experience with specialized research and
analysis won't even know what competent expertise *feels* like. It's
not a new idea. Liu Shao, writing about human relations management in China, said it seventeen hundred years ago: "You cannot
recognize in another a quality you do not have yourself."

An Exciting Profession

Each of us has known some people who would pass the tests implied
in what I have written about the generalist role, about integrative
thinking, about making what hasn't happened before happen now.
Indeed, in any successful effort, from a summer camp to a television
show to a corporate merger to a peacetime alliance, you will find
working generalists near the center of activity. They are the people
who furnish most of the glue that holds people together and the
imagination around which other people mobilize.

Most of them might even object at first if you were to call them
leaders; they describe themselves, and their peers describe them, as
camp counselors, artists, businesspeople, or diplomats. But their
common talisman is *their concern for the general outcome*—and their
willingness to do something about that concern.

Paradoxically, the leaders who listen most attentively to what
our Declaration of Independence calls "the general opinion of

mankind" may seem (to their peers, to the establishment, to the media, and even to members of the general public for whom they purport to speak and act) to be uttering heretical thoughts, pre-scribing for undiagnosed diseases, proposing bizarre solutions—because others have not exercised the wider curiosity or done the integrative thinking that come more naturally to the generalist.

"Getting it all together" can be an exciting profession, but it can also be a vulnerable one. The first reaction to your good idea may recall that pungent line from a Ring Lardner story: "'Shut up,' my father explained." The resistance to what has never been done before may remind the generalist of Peter Ustinov's claim that one of his grade-school teachers wrote on his report card, "Peter shows great originality, which must be curbed at all costs." The first birds off the telephone wire (the image is John Gardner's) need both spunk and persistence.

Each of us who presumes to the kind of leadership that welcomes innovation while it is still new has to try hard to think about what the Club of Rome called the *problématique*, the constantly chang-ing general context. I mean this quite literally. None of us can expect to *act* on more than a tiny corner of the great complexity. But in our interrelated society, itself part of an uncompromisingly interdependent world, we have to *think* about the whole complex-ity in order to act relevantly on any part of it. A 1980 convention of futurists in Toronto summed up the generalist mandate in four now-famous words: "Think Globally, Act Locally."

The message comes through, loud and clear, from the most prophetic of our contemporary public philosophers. In one of his many lucid and useful books, *Managing in Turbulent Times*, Peter Drucker poses the puzzle of pluralism: "Each institution pursues its own specific goal. But who then takes care of the common weal?" His answer (and mine) is: the specialized professional who gradu-ates into general leadership. "He does not cease to be a 'profes-sional'; he must not cease to be one. But he acquires an additional dimension of understanding, additional vision, and the sense of responsibility for the survival and performance of the whole that distinguishes the manager from the subordinate and the citizen from the subject."

Scary as it is to be a citizen-leader so defined, we have to agree with John Gardner's exhortation (in a pithy little piece called "The War of the Parts Against the Whole"). This is a moment, he writes,

> when the innumerable interests, organizations and groups that make up our national life must keep their part of the bargain with the society that gives them freedom, by working toward the common good. Right now. In this time of trouble. Their chances for long-term enjoyment of pluralism will be enhanced by a long-term commitment to the common good as we go through this difficult passage. At least for now, a little less *pluribus*, a lot more *unum*.

It's not an easy philosophy. But don't blame the messengers who bring the news, blame the delightful complexities and stimulating dynamics of a society in rapid transition. And be assured, by one who has been there, that the exhilaration usually exceeds the exhaustion.

Commentary on Chapter Two

"The organizations that get things done will no longer be hierarchical pyramids with most of the real control at the top. They will be systems—interlaced webs of tension in which control is loose, power diffused, and centers of decision plural. 'Decision-making' will become an increasingly intricate process of multilateral brokerage. . . . Because organizations will be more horizontal, the way they are governed is likely to be more collegial, consensual, and consultative. The bigger the problems . . . the more real power is diffused and the larger the number of persons who can exercise it—if they work at it. This trend is visible in totalitarian as well as democratic societies. 'Collective leadership' and committee work are not conclusive evidence of democratic feelings. They are imperatives of bigness and complexity."

When those words of mine were published (*The Future Executive,* Harper & Row, 1972), I didn't know that, elsewhere in the United States, Dee Hock was organizing VISA International in what he came to call a *chaordic* (chaotic plus ordered) fashion. Getting to know him in recent years, and recently becoming a trustee of The Chaordic Commons, I have found that my way of thinking meshes closely with his.

During 2000, I tried to sum up in several articles and published interviews the essence of what I had often called uncentralized systems, using the VISA story as a leading case in point. *Public Administration Review, Inner Edge,* New Dimensions Radio, *The Futurist,* and *Perspectives* (journal of the World Business Academy) all published different versions of this line of thought. This essay is based on the text that appeared in *Perspectives,* December 2000—with some additions, updates, clarifications, and refinements.

2

Coming Soon

The Nobody-in-Charge Society

A Fusion of Chaos and Order

"If you think you can't, why think?"

This can-do aphorism comes from the pioneer who helped invent, then brought to stunning success, the remarkably uncentralized enterprise called VISA International.

Philosopher-executive Dee Hock, a local banker in Seattle, had been brooding for years about why modern institutions seemed to depend so much on "compelled behavior," which he considered a "disguised form of tyranny." "The organization of the future," he had come to believe, "will be the embodiment of *community* based on *shared purpose* calling to the *higher aspirations of people.*"

Most of us who ponder walking-in-the-woods thoughts like these don't get to try them on for size in the real world. But through a series of improbable accidents this small-bank vice president got a chance to organize a deliberately uncentralized company that, three decades later, now handles the world's largest block of consumer purchasing power.

Owned by more than 21,000 financial institutions operating in 220 countries and territories, the "products" of VISA International are used by more than a billion consumers at some 22 million locations to purchase nearly $2 *trillion* in goods and services. And during its first three decades, it has grown by 20 to 50 percent a year.

Hock is now promoting a new vocabulary to help us talk about how to organize without centralizing. His keyword is "chaord," a fusion of *chaos* and *order*. His 1999 book, *Birth of the Chaordic Age*, tells the dramatic story of VISA's origins. He doesn't claim VISA as a model. But it stands as a very large and very successful example of some very practical ideas about human organization that will, I believe, come to characterize the twenty-first century.

The Age of Pyramids

In the century we just said goodbye to, we learned again and again that complex social systems work badly if they are too centralized. In managing its agriculture, the Soviet Union put this proposition on public display for two-thirds of the twentieth century.

Yet for most twentieth-century people, the image of "good organization" was still a pyramid. In government, the pyramid's top was typically stuffed with political appointees, with serried ranks of civil servants—that is, servants expected to be civil to politicians—arranged in hierarchical fashion below.

In military organizations, of course, hierarchy had long been regarded as functional. In corporations also, organization charts were drawn as pyramids, following Max Weber's model of bureaucracy. Nonprofit agencies usually did likewise; they assumed that organizations making a profit must be doing something right.

Organized religion had likewise developed hierarchical trappings—that's what the word *organized* was taken to mean. Holy men (and in some denominations, grudgingly, holy women) were up front in the pulpit; affluent laypersons served as middle managers; parishioners in the pews were expected to be religious but not necessarily organized. Labor unions, despite their more egalitarian vocabulary, often had the look and feel of pyramids. And so did many social service agencies—though few went so far as the Salvation Army did in using military titles and uniforms.

In every kind of organization, the people at the "top" were paid more, and had larger offices and expense accounts, than their "subordinates." (The exceptions, publicity heroes in professional athletics and the movies, were dramatic but few.) Even in hospitals and universities and movie studios and publishing houses, where physicians and professors and creative artists and writers instinctively resisted the notion that they were rank-ordered middle managers, the language used to differentiate functions often sounded more hierarchical than collegial.

Pyramids Are Un-American

Opting for pyramids as the "natural" form of organization might seem natural in some European, Japanese, and other cultures once long submissive to monarchs or emperors governing by a mixture of divine right and military readiness. The founding fathers of the United States of America had something very different in mind. They were themselves undeniably upper-class, some even slaveholders. But the rhetoric of their Revolution had broken loose from hierarchies of right and might; it was full of inalienable rights and populist righteousness.

These leaders of an underdeveloped colony declared our eighteenth-century independence in human-rights language that much of the world caught up with only in the twentieth—under the leadership of that woman-of-the-century, Eleanor Roosevelt— and leaders in some parts of the world haven't yet understood.

Then they drafted a Constitution that departed dramatically from the oppressive pyramids the colonists had fled and learned to despise. Indeed, they created the basis for a nobody-in-charge society—quite literally a first-time experiment in uncentralized governance.

The "separation of powers," with its "checks and balances" and judicial review, was explicitly designed to deny any part of our federal government the chance to make too much yardage at the expense of the other parts—and of the people it was supposed to serve. The federal system itself was designed to create a continuous tussle between the states and the central government. The tussle was intended to be permanent; no part of the federal system was supposed to "win it all," not ever.

It is not just the durability of their extraordinary invention that testifies to the founders' wisdom. It is clear from the record they left that they—at least, the deepest thinkers among them, James Madison and Thomas Jefferson—knew just how unprecedented was the system they were proposing to build. The people were really *supposed* to be sovereign. Jefferson still believed this even after his eight years of trying, as president from 1801 to 1809, to be their "servant leader": "I know of no safe depository of the ultimate powers of the society but the people themselves," Thomas Jefferson wrote to a friend in 1820, "and if we think them not enlightened enough to exercise their control with a wholesome discretion, the remedy is not to take it from them, but to inform their discretion."

What's truly astonishing is that now, at the beginning of this new century, the practical prospect for a workable world seems to lie in reinventing their nobody-in-charge concept for *global* application.

The real-life management of peace worldwide seems bound to require a Madisonian world of bargains and accommodations among national and functional factions, a world in which people are able to agree on what to do next together without feeling the need (or being dragooned by some global government) to agree on religious creeds, economic canons, or political credos. A practical pluralism, not a unitary universalism, is the likely destiny of the human race.

For our present purpose, my point is simply that pyramid-building was always, and still is, essentially un-American. The real American tradition calls for the invention of systems in which nobody is in general charge—and, in consequence, each citizen is partly in charge.

The Spread of Uncentralization

That authentic tradition began to take hold of our destiny in the second half of the twentieth century. Just below the surface in every kind of organization, something important was happening, something very different from the vertical practice—recommendations up, orders down—of both public administration and business management. The "bright future for complexity," foretold in a 1927 *New Yorker* story by E. B. White, was coming to pass in the United States—prodded and speeded by the modern miracles of information technology.

The sheer complexity of what had to get done—by governments and corporations, but also by their myriad contractors and subcontractors and their nonprofit critics and cheerleaders—required huge numbers of people to exercise independent judgment, think for themselves, and consult with each other, *not* just "do as you're told."

The marriage of computers and telecommunications multiplied the speed and extended to global range financial speculation, business transactions, military operations, political dissidence, and humanitarian activity. And the widening access to information about what's happening, about who is doing what to whom and when and where, brought into financial markets and business decisions and military strategy and political protest and even humanitarian relief a host of kibitzers, lobbyists, and second-guessers who knew so much—or could readily discover it on the Internet—that they had to be taken into account.

There were still, to be sure, distinctions between organizations where the style of management is looser and more collegial and others where recommendations mostly go up and orders mostly come down. But by the end of the century, *all* kinds of organizations—from Marine platoons to urban hospitals—were moving away from vertical administration toward more consultative styles of operation.

The century just past thus opened a widening contrast between how organizations were described and how they really worked. So naturally, the search has been on for alternatives to *centralization* as an organizing concept. The first and seemingly obvious candidate was *decentralization*.

Most of the central administrators who opted to *decentralize* found, to their satisfaction, that this was a new way to preserve hierarchy. If things were becoming so complicated that grandpa could no longer understand it all, he could still subdivide and parcel out all the *work* to be done—while hanging onto central control with more and more creative accounting systems. Decentralization thus became an aspect, indeed a subhead, of centralization.

The real opposite of centralization is of course *uncentralization*. Mao Tse-tung played with this idea for a time; he called it "many flowers blooming." Then he pulled back when it became clear that if China really permitted people's free exercise of opinion and initiative, the Communist Party's central control would be the first casualty.

Meanwhile, the underlying American bias favoring looser systems—featuring personal initiative, voluntary cooperation, joint ventures, committee work, and networking—was being reinforced by the dazzling progress of information technology and its impact on everything from preschool education to the understanding of our universe.

Very large systems, many of them global in scale, based on massive information outputs and widespread feedback, have been developed in the twentieth century. Global information systems unimaginable before the marriage of computers and telecommunications—currency and commodity markets, epidemic controls, automatic banking, worldwide credit cards, airline and hotel reservation systems, global navigation guidance, and the World Weather Watch come readily to mind—now seem normal, almost routine. It is no accident of history that American imagination and leadership were a priceless ingredient in developing each of these systems.

In all these cases, there are commonly agreed standards, plus a great deal of uncentralized discretion. The same is true, even more true, of the international foreign exchange market and the Internet, now the world's two most pervasive nobody-in-charge systems. Their common standards so far are mostly technical. Ethical standards for global human behavior await the social inventors of the twenty-first century.

The Role of Mutual Adjustment

If all organizations are becoming "nobody-in-charge systems," how will anything get done? How *will* we get everybody in on the act, and still get some action?

We will do it, I think, by creating systems that manage to minimize, and clearly define, what everybody must agree on—common norms and standards—and in all other matters maximize each participant's opportunity and incentive to use common sense, imagination, and suasive skills to advance the organization's common purpose.

This means, of course, that those who are going to pursue an organization's purpose together have to be openly consulted about the purpose, not only about the means of its pursuit.

Wisdom about uncentralized systems thus starts with a simple observation: most of what each of us does from day to day does *not* happen because someone told us to do it.

When you walk along a city street, you don't collide with other pedestrians; you, and they, instinctively avoid bumping into each other. To generalize: any human system that works is working because nearly all of the people involved in it cooperate to make sure that it works.

Political scientist Charles Lindblom called this *mutual adjustment:* in a generally understood environment of moral rules, norms, conventions, and mores, very large numbers of people can watch each other, then modify their own behavior just enough to accommodate the differing purposes of others but not so much that the mutual adjusters lose sight of where they themselves want to go.

Imagine a large clump of people on either side of a busy downtown intersection, waiting for the traffic light to change before crossing the street. There is *macro* discipline here. The convention of the red light means the same thing—danger—to all the participants in this complexity, even though there is no physical barrier to violating the norm at their own risk. Then the light turns green. It would be theoretically possible, with the help of a sizable staff of computer analysts, to chart in a central *micro* plan the ideal passageways that would enable each pedestrian to get to the other sidewalk without bumping into any other pedestrian. But not even the most totalitarian systems have tried to plan in such detail.

What works is mutual adjustment: somehow those two knots of people march toward each other and there are no collisions. Each person adjusts to the others, yet all reach their objective—a "positive-sum game" if there ever was one.

A Drifting Barge

It is not only at street corners that mutual adjustment works. It works also in global markets. Even in markets dominated by cartels or would-be monopolists, most decisions are not made by authorities giving orders. Prices serve as an information feedback system that instructs people all over the world how to adjust their behavior to take advantage of the system. Quite literally, no one is in charge.

No national government now controls the value of its own money. Banks in Europe and elsewhere create dollars as required, lots of them, without so much as a curtsy to Washington, D.C. The international monetary system—as free as a market can be, already out of national control, not yet under international control—is chronically at risk of a nervous breakdown.

In the first half of the half-century after World War II, the monetary system had a measure of stability—that is, companies and countries knew roughly what their money would be worth in other countries because exchange rates among all currencies were pegged to the price of gold by international agreement (the Bretton Woods agreement, administered by the International Monetary Fund). But once the United States, and soon everyone else, got off that train in 1971, currencies started to float in their comparative values. From then on, what each major country's money was worth (compared to other nations' money) mostly depended on how well it managed its own affairs: nursed its growth rate, kept its budget near balance, avoided too much inflation, recovered handily from recessions.

Market increasingly means *international*. The earlier, more successful deals, among fewer countries, to dismantle obstacles to commerce, under the General Agreement on Tariffs and Trade (GATT), helped the volume of trade across frontiers to grow by as much as 500 percent between 1950 and 1975, while the increase in global output was growing less than half as fast, by about 220 percent. This meant that theoretically national economies were increasingly beyond the reach of presidents and prime ministers, parliaments and congresses, or even the formerly powerful central bankers.

Since nobody could manage the system, such policymaking as was attempted occurred in talks among governments, especially those governing the biggest economies with the most sought-after currencies. Trade experts at GATT in Geneva hammered out international codes and rules. Finance ministers lectured each other about the dangers of inflation. Central bankers intervened in the money markets in mostly ineffectual efforts to prop up the value of their own, and sometimes other countries', currencies.

The heads of the seven biggest industrial democracies (Britain, Canada, France, Germany, Italy, Japan, and the United States), latterly joined by Russia, gathered in summit meetings to pretend that they were steering the global barge. Meanwhile the barge, loose from its moorings and unresponsive to its helm, was adrift in the crosscurrents and riptides created by millions of buyers and sellers in largely unregulated worldwide markets for things, services, information, and money.

Common Sense and Common Safety

What enables mutual adjustment to work is the wide availability of relevant information, so each mutual adjuster can figure out what the others might do under varied conditions, and give forth useful signals for them to use in turn.

Perhaps the best current example of mutual adjustment at work is the Internet—at least on a good day. People all over the world are exchanging information, images, music, and voice messages, with so little regulation that their commerce is often noncommercial, in effect a multilateral barter system. Many of their transactions are essentially not exchange but *sharing* arrangements. Where there are rules of behavior, they are increasingly arrived at by consensus among the participants, or at least ratified in action by those who will be guided by them.

That doesn't mean the rule-abiding citizens are serfs, doing some lord's bidding. If the rules work, it's because nearly all those who need to abide by them are motivated to comply because the rules make sense to them. In the developing culture of the World Wide Web, there are more and more examples of enforcement by peer pressure—large numbers of people exercising their privilege of excluding messages from ill-mannered participants or refusing to do business with individuals or Web sites they regard as untrustworthy, and telling each other when they make such decisions.

Even in mutual-adjustment systems that provide for compulsion by police power, that power often remains latent. In the United States, there are laws about driving on the right-hand side of the road. The laws are ultimately enforced by the state's police power. But if you don't agree with the rule and try instead to drive to the left, you are quite likely to get killed well before the police arrive to enforce compliance. So, as a matter of common sense and common safety, you drive to the right. The effective enforcement is not the state's authority, it's the shared opinion of your neighbors with whom you share the public right-of-way.

Setting International Standards

The truth here arrives, as truth usually does, in a small, paradoxical package: The key to a genuinely *uncentralized* system is mutually agreed standards on whatever is *central* to the system and thus cannot be left to individual choices or market outcomes.

In some ways the most dramatic, and least remarked, nobody-in-charge system is the way international standards are already set for many thousands of products and services.

It started in 1906, with engineers trying to make sure that "electrotechnical" gadgets would fit together and work the way they were supposed to work, anywhere in the world. Other engineers picked up the idea in some other fields. But it wasn't until after World War II, in 1947, that an International Organization for Standardization was formed.

The organization is called ISO. That's not an acronym, which wouldn't work for a multilingual club anyway. Derived from the Greek *isos*, meaning "equal," it's the root of the prefix *iso-* that occurs in many words such as *isometric* (of equal measure or dimensions), *isodynamic* (having the same strength or intensity), and *isonomy* (equality of political rights). As ISO's Web site puts it: "From 'equal' to 'standard,' the line of thinking that led to the choice of 'ISO' as the name of the organization is easy to follow."

The first ISO standard, a "reference temperature for industrial length measurement," was published in 1951. Half a century later, there are now 13,544 International Standards, recorded on 403,608 pages. This standard-setting effort, coordinated by a nongovernment from a headquarters in Switzerland, costs less than $90,000,000 a year and engages the efforts of some 30,000 "experts on loan," working as equal partners in 2,885 committees and working groups, in a wide variety of technical fields. Their commonsense approach has been summed up this way: "Do it once, do it right, do it internationally."

ISO standards are *voluntary*—that is, enforced in the marketplace: if you produce something fastened by screws that aren't standard, the word will get around fast and customers will shun you. They are *industrywide*, designed to provide global solutions to satisfy suppliers and consumers worldwide. And they are developed *by consensus*.

That doesn't mean they need unanimous consent. An ISO standard can be adopted if it is approved by two-thirds of those actively involved and is blessed by three-quarters of the ISO members— national standard-setting bodies—that vote. Maybe they don't even need voting rules, just the definition of *consensus* I found useful long ago while practicing multilateral diplomacy at the U.N. and in NATO: "the acquiescence of those who care [about each particular decision], supported by the apathy of those who don't."

Once international standards are set—for metric screw threads, for bolts, for welding, for electronic data processing, for paper sizes, for automobile control symbols, for the safety of wire ropes, for film speed codes, for freight containers, and even for country names, currencies, and languages—a genuinely free market is possible. Competition within the rules of the game can be free and fair—and markets that are both free and fair are likely to grow faster than others.

The three VISA cards I carry in my wallet look very much alike—the magnetic code is in a predictable place on each card—because they adhere to an ISO standard. The three financial institutions that issued them cooperated on that, but now they happily compete for my custom—happily, because each is operating in a much larger market than any of them could reach if they hadn't first cooperated with each other.

The Uncentralization Path

It may be helpful to sum up—and thus oversimplify—the rationale for the uncentralized systems that I believe will be more and more characteristic of the post-postmodern era now ahead of us:

- For any complex activity to run in an uncentralized manner, there have to be some rules of the game (like the ISO standards).

- The rules need to be adopted by a sufficiently participatory, or representative, process, that nearly all the followers feel they have been part of the leadership.

- Until the rules are truly acceptable shared doctrine, there will need to be some authority (a police officer at an urban intersection, a boss in a company, a guru in an ashram, a parent in a family) to remind everybody about the agreed rules.

- In time, the rules become internalized standards of behavior—and the resulting community doesn't need anybody to be in charge.

- The rules are then learned at a parent's knee or at school or by adult experience and informal (but effective) peer pressure. Procedural reminders and consequent services can mostly be automated—as with signal lights for automobile traffic and ATMs for routine banking.

In every well-functioning market, most of those involved in the myriad transactions are able to buy when they want to buy and sell when they want to sell, precisely *because* no one is in charge. The discipline is provided by wide and instant knowledge of the prevailing price of whatever is sought or offered.

The uncentralized way of thinking and working naturally becomes more complicated as civilization moves from the small homogeneous village to large multicultural societies, and beyond that to the governance of communities in cyberspace.

But there is, I believe, a path from the need for standards, through the practice of consensus and the constituting of interim authorities (whose mandate is to work themselves out of their interim jobs), to patterns of naturally cooperative behavior—a path that is equally valid for organized human effort however complex it has to be.

Releasing Human Ingenuity

How to conceive, plan, organize, and lead human institutions in ways that best release human ingenuity and maximize human choice is one of the great conundrums of the century now ahead of us.

The long-ago philosophy and recent history of the United States provide useful hints for people who bring other people together in

organizations to make something different happen. This is a game
anyone can play. Here, for starters, are some hints from my own
experience:

- No individual can be truly "in general charge" of anything interesting or important. That means everyone
  involved is partly in charge. How big a part each participant plays will much depend on how responsible
  he or she feels for the general outcome of the collective effort.

- Broader is better. The more people affected by a decision feel they were consulted about it, the more likely
  it is that the decision will stick.

- Looser is also better. The fewer and narrower are the
  rules that *everyone* involved must follow, the more
  room there is for individual discretion and initiative,
  small-group insights and inventions, regional adaptations, functional variations. Flexibility and informality
  are good for coworkers' morale, constituency support,
  investor enthusiasm, customer satisfaction.

- Planning is not architecture, it's more like fluid drive.
  Real-life planning is improvisation on a general sense
  of direction—announced by the few perhaps, but only
  after genuine consultation with the many who will
  need to improvise on it.

- Information is for sharing, not hoarding. Planning
  staffs, systems analysis units, and others whose full-
  time assignment is to think, shouldn't report only
  in secret to some boss. Their relevant knowledge has
  to be shared, sooner rather than later, with all those
  who might be able to use it to advance the organization's purpose.

Some years ago Japanese auto companies—advised by a genius engineer from Michigan—started sharing much more information on productivity with workers on the assembly lines. Small groups of workers on the factory floor, reacting to that information, were able to think up countless little changes that increased speed, cut costs, improved quality, enhanced productivity. Quite suddenly, Japanese autos became globally supercompetitive.

Add your own hints-from-experience, to taste.

Symbols, Not Things

The rapid drift toward uncentralized systems is not a temporary aberration from some centralized norm. It is happening because information has recently become the world's dominant resource— and because information is fundamentally different from land, minerals, energy, and other physical resources that have played the starring role in world history.

Centralized hierarchies were in the nature of *things*. But information is symbols, not things. Uncentralized networks are the "appropriate technology" for management in a symbols environment.

The direction of this change was already becoming obvious during the latter part of the twentieth century. Everywhere, we saw a shift from top-down vertical relationships toward more horizontal, consensual, collaborative modes of organizing. The best leaders in this new century will be those who learn, early and often, how to fuse chaos and order in uncentralized systems.

I don't know whether Dee Hock's intriguing word *chaordic* will make it into the next edition of my favorite dictionary. I hope it does. But what I'm sure about is this: the wave he is surfing has already rolled powerfully into this, the Global Century.

With every generation of information technology—that is, every two or three years—our future becomes more uncentralized. That has to be good news—for individual creativity and invention, for personal freedom, for human choice. Let's make the most of it.

Commentary on Chapter Three

In the autumn of 1998 the World Academy of Art and Science held its largest and most ambitious assembly ever. Hosted by Canadian Fellows in Vancouver, B.C., the gathering went by the name of The Global Century.

At the threshold of a new millennium, I then wrote, "we look out at a world swept by waves of change that erode all ways of thinking that hold any special peoples, in regions defined by geography or wealth or even by military technology, as having a manifest destiny to lead. Nor can any people defined by historical tradition, ethnicity, culture, or belief presume to be 'in charge.' The relevant 'region' now seems to be the whole world we inhabit together. The term 'global citizen,' once put down as impractical idealism, now seems an accurate way to describe each of us."

Thereafter Zia Sardar, editor of the British journal *Futures* and a World Academy Fellow, used the same theme to plan a double issue of his journal for November-December 1999. Its contents were papers written by Fellows from four continents. Walter Truett Anderson (in 2001 my successor as president of the World Academy) and I edited the issue.

My lead essay for that end-of-century volume was focused, as this book is, on the complex intermesh of the Information Revolution, the consequent spread of knowledge, and the huge impact of these developments on the practice of leadership. Much of what is happening—and is going to happen—can be explained by the *nature* of information, now the world's dominant resource, and how it is converted by the human brain and spirit into usable knowledge and practical wisdom.

We obviously need some general theory about this new environment in which information leads to knowledge and, if we're lucky, to wisdom too.

3

The Spread of Knowledge

Ten Interactive Revolutions

On this first day of the rest of our lives, it may be useful to raise our periscopes for a 360-degree look around. My sweep of the horizon shows ten worldwide revolutions transforming our world. They are concurrent but not parallel—rather, they are intermixed, interwoven, interactive.

- *First.* The sudden increase in explosive power has clamped a lid on the scale of warfare—a first in human history. The invention of weapons too big for states to use converted much of big-power military strategy into an expensive information game. But it also leaves smaller wars in scattered places and big explosions set off in crowded places by nongovernments as the archetypal riddles of "global security" in the twenty-first century.

- *Second.* Biotechnology, including the deciphering of information in living genes, presents humankind with a vast range of new ethical and political puzzles. Human cloning and stem-cell research, which have recently captured the headlines, are only two of them. In all sorts of ways, what we human beings do or decide not to do increasingly determines our own evolution—and that of all the other living species with which we share a common biosphere.

- *Third*. Computers, serving as prosthetic extensions of our brainpower, are replacing much of the repetitious drudgery people have always had to endure. They bring in their train new puzzles about the future of work. But the elimination of drudgery can't be bad news for the generations to come.

- *Fourth*. Linking fast computers with more reliable telecommunications enables us to model and simulate vast systems such as the global atmosphere, the human genome, and nuclear fallout from megaton explosions. This sensitizes us to the consequences of what we the people are doing to our natural environment—and might inadvertently do to ourselves.

- *Fifth*. The widening spread of knowledge is leading to a fundamental change in the technology of organization: pyramids and command-and-control operations are on their way out, consultation and consensus are increasingly "in."

These five transformations are driven quite directly by scientific discovery and technological innovation. The other five are facilitated, even intensified, by science and technology. But they are *driven* by universal aspirations of the human spirit—by a widespread sense of entitlement to "enough" (the fulfillment of basic human needs), and beyond that by equally basic human desires for a sense of achievement, justice, solidarity, and participation.

- *Sixth*. The idea of human rights for everyone has become the world's first truly universal idea-system. It has come to mean rights not only for recognized minorities and political prisoners, but also for women, children, and the aging, for racial and ethnic minorities, for immigrants, for refugees, and for all manner of people once considered untouchables. Matching universal human rights with universal human responsibilities, however, has been left to be worked out in the twenty-first century.

- *Seventh.* A global fairness revolution is spreading as the spread of knowledge shows the disadvantaged in every society what they are missing—and provides them with new means of communication to express their rising resentments and help them "overcome."

- *Eighth.* Fierce loyalties to cultural identity with less-than-global communities—bonded by nationhood, ethnicity, race, religion, ideology, and even occupation—are colliding everywhere with the homogenizing cultures of so-called modernization.

- *Ninth.* An emerging ethic of ecology is producing a revolution in human self-control—based not on "limits to growth" but on limits to thoughtlessness, unfairness, and conflict. The resulting international cooperation is producing, here and there, a "growth of limits."

- *Tenth.* Openness, market incentives, and the practice of pluralism are currently on display in some of the unlikeliest places. Authoritarian and totalitarian systems are simply unable to compete with looser systems that "go with the flow" in the global flood of knowledge.

These global tides and currents are all related to each other. Indeed, modern biologists and ecologists have joined a long list of spiritual prophets, inspired poets, and secular philosophers in insisting that everything is related to everything else, that human beings are all somehow connected to each other—and that, in consequence, each of us has to try and think hard about the situation as a whole.

Many of these changes-in-progress are touched on in the writings gathered in this volume. But what may, as a scientist might say, get lost in the noise is the reason for it all: the historically sudden spread of knowledge, that huge transformation underdescribed by the pallid phrase *the Information Revolution*.

The Information Environment

I learned in Hawaii, where I once lived in the shadow of a volcano, that long before the top blows off, seismologists can hear the volcano clearing its throat. In trying to detect the seismic rumbling of our human futures, we social nonscientists also learn to look for relevant clues. Among our clues are the tools humans fashion ahead of the eruptions that follow—because our tools are typically invented *before* we can imagine how they will be used.

Scientists who study animals suggest that it's not quite clear that humans are in all respects brighter than some animals—brainier than dolphins, say. But it's surely clear from our short history on this planet that humans are much better than dolphins, or chimpanzees or elephants, at making tools. We mounted an agricultural revolution with "the plow that broke the Plains." We invented motors and brought forth the Industrial Revolution. And just the other day, we did it again.

In the great social event of the 1980s, we married computers to electronic communications and touched off another eruption of change that will affect everybody and everything—every political process, every business, every profession, every intellectual discipline, every "settled" theory, every organized religion, every traditional culture—in the Global Century.

We cannot pretend to forecast just *what* will happen, or *when*. But we already know something more important: *why* it will happen.

As far into the future as we can see, information will be playing the lead role in world history that physical labor, stone, bronze, land, minerals, metals, and energy once played. That requires us, who are destined to live in the twenty-first century, to revise all sorts of assumptions we have treated as solid but now turn out to be fragile and flawed.

We have to burn into our consciousness how very different information is from all its predecessors as civilization's dominant resource—because information is *symbols*, not things. The essence of this difference is that information is more accessible—to all sorts of people in all kinds of ways—than the world's dominant resource has ever been before.

If information—refined by rational thinking into knowledge, converted by both intuition and reasoning into wisdom—is now the world's crucial resource, what does that portend for the future? Thinking hard about the inherent characteristics of information provides valuable clues to what lies ahead.

Information expands as it's used. This proposition has been winning reluctant but widening acceptance since John McHale advanced it in 1972 in his landmark book, *The Changing Information Environment*.

Some information is certainly depletive over time. A tip on the fourth race at Belmont might be valuable at lunchtime and valueless by dinnertime. Yesterday's forecast of today's weather is of merely historical interest tomorrow. But for the most part, as Anne Wells Branscomb has written, information is "a synergistic resource . . . the more we have the more we use and the more useful it becomes."

Information is consequently not scarce. Because it is expandable without any obvious limits, the facts are never all in—and data are available in such profusion that uncertainty becomes the most important planning factor. The further a society moves toward making its living from the analysis and manipulation of information, the more its citizens will be caught up in a continual struggle to reduce the information overload on their desks and in their lives in order to reduce the uncertainty about what to *do*.

In the information society, we trade glut for scarcity, flood for drought. But *information-rich* doesn't mean *affluent*; it is quite as likely to mean *swamped*. We know from experience that, in nature, too much is often as troublesome as too little; poverty and misery can result from either drought or flood. We are all learning, or trying to learn, to deal with information entropy—that is, uncertainty caused by too much information.

The ultimate limits to growth of knowledge and wisdom are time (available to human minds for reflecting, analyzing, and integrating the information that is "brought to life" by being used), and the capacity of people—individually and in groups—to think integratively. There are obvious limits to the time each of us can devote to the production of knowledge, the sparkle of intuition, and the refinement of wisdom. But the capacity of humanity to integrate its collective experience through relevant individual thinking is expandable, if not without limits, at least within limits we cannot now measure or even imagine.

Information is transportable—at almost the speed of light, and through telepathy and prayer, much faster than that. In the past century, we have been witness to a major dimensional change in both the speed and volume of human activity, a change in transportability of resources greater than the multimillennial shift from foot travel to the supersonic jet.

As a result, for more and more of the world's people, remoteness is now more a matter of choice than of geography. Already during the past decade and a half, it has been possible for you to sit anywhere there is a workable telephone service and trade on the New York stock markets in real time, though in some time zones you might have to keep rather peculiar hours. There is now no inherent reason for a stock exchange to be in a traditional "financial center." Many years ago Citicorp located its whole credit card operation in a place in South Dakota that is "remote" only by preelectronic standards.

With the passing of remoteness, "distance learning" has now become a major business in many parts of the world. Like all new fashions, it has its limits; computer-assisted communication is not a substitute for face-to-face contact. But the converse is equally true.

Once I get to know you pretty well, up close and personal, I really don't need to see your face every time we talk on the phone or exchange messages by e-mail. What's clear now is that combining up-close and distance learning enhances the educational experience beyond what is possible with either mode alone.

Seventeen years ago, I was writing a book about all this on a laptop in Punalu'u on the Big Island of Hawaii, in order to "get away from it all." At the same time and from the same cottage, I was conducting a computer teleconference on leadership with three dozen business executives scattered from Seattle to Abu Dhabi—with whom I had become acquainted at a week-long seminar in La Jolla, arranged by the Western Behavioral Sciences Institute. (And I'm very far from being a "pro" in information technology; I always seem to be panting several steps behind the latest computer upgrade or wireless gadgetry.) In the world of information-richness, you will still be able to be remote—but you will have to work at it.

Information leaks. It *tends* to leak, and the more it leaks the more we have and the more of us have it. Information is aggressive, even imperialistic, in striving to break out of the unnatural bonds of secrecy in which thing-minded people try to imprison it. Like a virus (itself a tiny information system), information tries to affect the organisms around it. The straitjackets of public secrecy, intellectual property rights, and confidentiality of all kinds fit very loosely on this restless resource.

In practice—as distinguished from law—information cannot really be owned; only its delivery service can. The resulting confusion undermines the whole idea of "intellectual property," which is clearly an oxymoron, a contradiction in terms. It is, of course, quite possible to encourage and reward creativity—it happens all the time in universities—without gluing creativity to the notion of personal property rights. Even now, most patents and copyrights are held in the names, not of individual creators, but of the companies, publishers, and government agencies for which they work—or used to work.

We will be wise, early in the twenty-first century, to invent, elaborate, and project a more viable concept that leaves plenty of room for *incentives for human creativity*, yet doesn't rest on "ownership of information" as its moral, economic, and philosophical basis. And the footings on which "trade secrecy" and government classification systems rest are just as vulnerable as patent and copyright law to the predictable tornadoes of change. They also deserve a skeptical new look early in the Global Century.

Information empowers the many. The spread of knowledge, the widening of educational opportunities, the proliferation of educated people around the world has made it harder and harder for power to be wielded by leaders on the grounds that they understand, let alone control, mysteries that are inaccessible to people in general. In the societies with the largest numbers of educated people, the spreading skepticism about authority figures—political leaders, corporate executives, media moguls, religious leaders, lawyers, physicians, scientists, and other experts—is overwhelmingly documented in survey research.

In the past three centuries, we have seen how aristocracies of achievement—upper classes empowered by their capacity to convert specialized kinds of knowledge into new kinds of wealth, notoriety, and political influence—took over from the older, narrower aristocracies of birth and landed wealth. In the second half of the twentieth century, we have seen the beginnings of another huge shift in influence.

As rich-poor gaps widen, the spread of knowledge also widens the constituencies of people who come to understand why the outcomes are so unfair. Often led by the educated young, they complain with increasing asperity about their exclusion from "the system," and wonder more and more loudly why they are not participating in its governance. The stunningly bloodless revolutions of 1989–1991 in Eastern Europe, the dissolution of the Soviet Union in 1991, and the sea-changes elsewhere thereafter bear witness.

When it comes to politics, people who think are notoriously ornery and inventive. It doesn't even seem to matter much what they have been educated to think about; part of what they learn in every field of knowledge is the joy of creative choice. If the freedom to choose is so clearly evident in their specialist learnings, it's no big step to the conviction that freedom of political choice is not only attractive but attainable. That's why the spread of education around the world eroded the pyramids of power and wealth and dis-crimination that looked like granite but turned out to be porous sandstone, crumbling under pressure.

Information is shared (not "exchanged"). In the 1970s I learned from the late great communications theorist, Professor Colin Cherry of the University of London, that information by its nature cannot give rise to exchange transactions, only to *sharing* transactions.

In a 1985 book I expressed this idea this way: "Things are exchanged: if I give you a flower or sell you my automobile, you have it and I don't. But if I sell you an idea, we both have it. And if I give you a fact or tell you a story, it's like a good kiss: sharing the thrill enhances it. Conversely, if the kiss carries a disease (informa-tion harmful to your mental health), the sharing transaction can be infectious." I could update this description by using as illustrations the sharing of computer software or popular music or genome research, but the principle would remain: if it's a thing, it's exchanged; if it's information, it's shared.

The difference is fundamental. It's what is inducing much rethinking of theory and practice, of law and custom, as we the peo-ple of every state, every nation, every government, every company, every kind of organization come to terms—gradually, as in any major cultural transformation—with the fact that the world's key resource is now a sharing resource.

Some Twenty-First-Century Conundrums

In sum: Information is not necessarily depletive; it expands as it's used. It is readily transportable, at close to the speed of light—or even faster. Information leaks so easily that it is much harder to hide and to hoard than tangible resources; it cannot be owned (though its delivery service can). The spread of information, converted into knowledge, empowers the many, by eroding the influence that once empowered the few who were "in the know." Giving or selling information is not an exchange transaction, it's a sharing transaction.

These five simple, pregnant propositions, as they sink in around the world and down the generations, should help us sort out some of the big conundrums that puzzle us as we set forth in the new millennium. For example:

The rapid globalization of ideas and markets—made possible by new information technologies—is no longer a policy option but a fact of life in the Global Century. During the last half of the twentieth century, the repetitive dramas of international finance, the burgeoning environmental movement, the emergence of world law, the epidemic spread of disease, the migration of people, the politics of the global commons, the world attention to local cultural collisions, have all been displayed in living color day and night on relentlessly global networks of electronic communication. Our widening awareness broadens our individual responsibility. If we are all connected and nobody can know enough to give orders, then each of us has some responsibility for the general outcome.

Diversity, it seems clear, will be the law of life on this planet. The more people learn about themselves and their neighbors, the more they can differentiate between "us" and "them." But with that knowledge comes also an acute awareness of commonalities and mutual interests, and the peril of focusing entirely on the differences—"clinging to their own roots and uprooting their neighbors' roots," as Thomas Friedman writes of the Middle East.

People will just have to find ways to be *different, yet together*— not only in the Balkans and the Middle East but in the many thousands of multiracial, multifaith communities around the world. And in matters that require common actions with global impact, such as arise in the oceans and the atmosphere, information technologies are coming onstream that will help hundreds of millions of very different peoples understand the need for common actions and common constraints.

The definition of community will have to expand. Down through history *community* has mostly meant the ties among people who lived or worked near each other. Even where a community's roots were in a common religion or ethnic identity, people identified most closely with the like-minded who were geographically close at hand. Now and in the future, the comparative ease of travel and communication makes it possible for *community* also, and increasingly, to mean people with similar interests and motivations who work and play together wherever they are living, working—or even traveling.

In an interconnected world economy that now changes with unprecedented speed, economic success comes not to those who do more and more of what they have already done well but to those who persist in doing what has never been done before. The pioneers in economic and social development will continue to find, however, that innovation is not the road to instant popularity.

Issues of economic fairness will become even more intense. One estimate is that at the start of the new century 1.5 billion people, a quarter of the world's population, were living on the equivalent of $1 or less a day. Another calculates that the richest 20 percent of the world's population consume 86 percent of global production, and the poorest 20 percent consume 1 percent.

What's new, compared to a hundred or even twenty-five years ago, is that as information leaks around the globe, very large numbers of people are learning about what goes on elsewhere—good things happening in places near and far that could happen to them if their leaders were wiser and more flexible, and bad things happening to other people that could spill over in their lives if they don't watch out.

For the nations that reached the status called developed *in the twentieth century, the premise of citizenship was that citizens had to be educated for self-government and socially useful skills.* Those societies bet heavily on universal elementary education, widespread secondary education, and advanced education and training for all who both merited and desired it. It is no accident that the countries that acted on that idea—and could afford to make that bet—are now the richer ones. (The most recent member of OECD, the "rich countries" club, is the Republic of Korea, an ex-colony that wagered on universal education only in 1950—because it had a technological war to fight—and then, prodded by the enthusiastic response of an education-hungry public, stuck with that policy for the ensuing half-century.)

The Twilight of Hierarchy

I will add just a word here about the changing seismology of leadership—the topic to which the essays in this volume are addressed. The shift is now more than obvious: from top-down vertical relationships toward horizontal, consensual, collaborative modes of getting people together to make something different happen. This seismic shift is also, very clearly, a consequence of the spread of information—symbols, not things—as the newly dominant resource.

It was in the nature of *things* that the few had access to key resources and the many did not: there never seemed to be enough to go around. The inherent characteristics of physical resources (the natural ones and those created by human ingenuity) made possible—perhaps even necessary—the development of hierarchies of five kinds: hierarchies of *power based on control* (of new weapons, of transport vehicles, of trade routes, or markets, and even of knowledge back when secrets could be secure), hierarchies of *influence based on secrecy*, hierarchies of *class based on ownership*, hierarchies of *privilege based on early access* to particular pieces of land or especially valuable resources, and hierarchies of *politics based on geography*.

Each of these five bases for hierarchy and discrimination was clearly crumbling in the waning years of the twentieth century. The old means of control were of dwindling efficacy. Secrets were harder and harder to keep (as the CIA and the White House seemed to have to relearn every few weeks). And ownership, early arrival, and geography were of declining importance in accessing, remembering, analyzing, and using the knowledge and wisdom that are the really valuable legal tender of our time.

The complexities of modern life, and the interconnectedness of everything to everything else, mean that in our communities, our nations, and our world, nobody can possibly know enough to be in general charge of anything important or interesting. This state of affairs is becoming more apparent with each passing year. It may be one reason why, more and more, the followers—especially university students and educated adults—seem so often to come forth with policy judgments while their established leaders are still making up their minds.

The twilight of hierarchy opens up a fast-growing requirement for people who can and will take the lead—and requires very different attitudes and strategies for those who opt to point the way. In modern societies many organizations still look like pyramids from a distance; but both their internal processes and their external relations feature much less command, much more consultation and consensus. That's what will require, for a constantly growing proportion of every citizenry, a wider-angle focus on the situation as a whole.

Commentary on Chapter Four

For most of my life, it has seemed clear that important issues of public policy are only decided after what John Gardner calls the "untidy and impressive" process of wide consultation. It makes sense, in a democracy, that a policy announcement should be made after, not before, most people affected by it have already made up their minds.

Yet I find that many leaders are called *policymakers.* They even act as though their utterances are the beginning, not the culmination, of policymaking. In the first years of the Clinton administration, huge amounts of time and effort were devoted to spelling out a universal health care system for the United States. But since most of the people, and the many special interests with a stake in the outcome, were not effectively consulted, all that effort went for naught.

The sudden spread of democracy in the closing years of the twentieth century found people who were thought of as followers in many places getting out ahead of their so-called leaders. And the global growth of civil society demonstrated the crucial role in policy-politics that has to be played by nongovernmental organizations.

The emergence of NGOs as major policy-influencing players in both domestic and international affairs is a huge and somewhat neglected story line—until one of them does something outrageous enough to rate a headline. It gets short shrift because most news and comment focuses so much attention on who's announcing government policy and so little on the complex processes by which the policy came to be announced.

I have talked and written a good deal about this over the years. This essay is a sampler, on a subject that everyone who takes the lead, on anything from now on, will do well to understand.

4

The Age of People-Power

We have it our power to begin the world all over
again. A situation similar to the present hath not
appeared since the days of Noah until now. The
birthday of a new world is at hand.

—*Thomas Paine, 1775*

Who Leads?

With perhaps a little less hyperbole, we now have every reason to feel as Paine did—if we take seriously the chances and choices just ahead, and we're willing to face up to the new kinds of threats and dangers we are also heir to, at this open moment in world affairs.

In the decade and more since the drama of Tiananmen Square in Beijing, the volcanic eruptions in the public squares of Eastern Europe, and the sudden bloodless collapse and dismemberment of the Soviet Union, the idea of political choice has been busting out all over. The right to choose was the dominant metaphor of the 1990s. The twenty-first century may prove to be the Age of People-Power, around the world and in the United States.

The first time that playwright Vaclav Havel visited the United States as president of a once-again democratic Czechoslovakia, he was asked on public television for his opinion, as a dramatist, of 1989's histrionics in Eastern Europe. "It was," he replied with unrehearsed eloquence, "a drama so thrilling and tragic and absurd that no earth-ling could have written it."

The drama's central lesson was clear enough: the people, not their leaders, were doing the leading. It's high time now to start digesting this lesson, and thinking hard about what it means for governance and peacebuilding in the twenty-first century.

That means not only thinking hard in the conventional categories of war and peace. It means rethinking who really makes policy in societies where knowledge has spread widely enough so most people think they should have a say in their own destiny. It also means feeling our way in the shadowy world where nongovernments can mobilize people-power to harass governments and corporations and take on more and more of the governance functions. And it will require hard thinking about how people-power can cope with the new kinds of threats epitomized by the leveling of the World Trade Center in New York City on September 11, 2001.

The People Out Ahead

Both the Soviet and Chinese strategies of reform-from-within were revolutions promoted—and, their leaders hoped—led from the top. But with the spread of knowledge, top-down reform will always be too little and too late. "The people" will all too easily get out ahead of the cautious reformers.

The bubbles of political choice rose and choked the old leaders of Eastern Europe. In the Soviet Union, the people's insistence on choice and self-determination developed a life of its own. In China a tight little group of lifetime associates, friends, and relations hung onto political power by opening the sluiceways of entrepreneurship and foreign economic relations. But a prudent oddsmaker would take bets not on whether they will be able to wall the government and the Communist Party off from the resulting winds of freedom but on when the people of the People's Republic will push their old political leaders into oblivion.

In the 1990s it was hard to think of a comparable time in world history when the political leaders of powerful countries seemed so irrelevant to important outcomes. Well-known names—presidents and prime ministers of the world's military powers and economic powerhouses—were staring at the nightly news with ill-concealed astonishment. One reason for the surprise was that this people-power had remarkably little to do with the customary measures of power: weapons, armed force, gross economic product. More than anything else, the power of ideas was in play.

The impatient crowds were moved not by distant visions of Utopia (which had been the Communists' stock-in-trade), but by spreading information about neighbors who were evidently getting more goods and services, more fairness in their distribution, and firmer guarantees of human rights than their own bosses and planners seemed able, or inclined, to deliver.

What caught up with Communist leaders in Eastern Europe and the Soviet Union was the contagion of what was happening in the democracies of Western Europe and North America. What is catching up with the rulers of China is unstoppable knowledge, especially among the educated young, of what is going on in South Korea, Taiwan, Hong Kong, and Singapore—and, at one remove, in Japan and the Western world.

The toughest dilemma top-down reformers face is how to educate people, especially young people, for the modern world without luring them into dissidence. It's a constant refrain in my writing, but worth repeating here: when it comes to politics, people who *think* are notoriously ornery and inventive. It doesn't even seem to matter much what they have been trained to think about; part of what they learn in every field of knowledge is the joy of creative choice. If freedom to choose is essential to their specialized studies, it's no big step to the conviction that freedom of political choice is not only attractive but attainable.

Reformers keep trying to draw a line between safe and unsafe learnings. A century ago, imperial China distinguished between "China's learning for essential matters" and "Western learning for practical matters." But how, these days, does one distinguish the practical from the essential, especially when the practical is so essential? A good deal of Western culture comes packaged with those so-called practical imports. Embedded in modern science and technology are Western notions about limits to government, about freedom to discover and experiment and innovate, about workers' rights, about managers' duty to lead without being bossy.

What's the lesson in all this for Americans in the twenty-first century? Don't cuddle up too close to reluctant reformers, who are slated nearly everywhere for early retirement. Bet instead on the power of democratic contagion, interacting with the bubble-up power of political choice.

Policymaking in America

Who really makes policy in the United States? Even in our pluralistic democracy, the notion that policy is made at the top, by well-known leaders, dies hard.

Some words of wisdom on this topic are contained—strangely enough—in the little red book, *The Thoughts of Chairman Mao Tse-tung,* which is no longer handed to foreigners who visit China. That booklet gathers between its covers a good deal of warmed-over Lenin, together with some editor's effort to rewrite nuggets of ancient Chinese wisdom and make them sound like Marxism. But the *Thoughts* also include a few passages of practical advice from a crafty and experienced leader who, like it or not, put together the largest revolution in world history.

In one of these passages, Mao is addressing the cadres (that is, the experts and community leaders) and he says, translated into American, something like this: Look, you cadres, don't get the idea that you're making the policy. The masses (that is, the people or the general public) are making the policy. Your job is to get out and sniff around (he doesn't mention scientific polling) and figure out where the people are going. Then you've got something to do that the people don't know how to do. You have to codify the policy, program and budget it, and organize staff to carry it out. But then you had better go back and check again with the people, to make sure that you keep up with their changing sense of direction. Then you recodify, reprogram, rebudget, reorganize. This "dialectic" between the leaders and the people, says Mao, is the correct theory of knowledge.

In his own backyard, Mao's rhetoric was way ahead of reality; it does not, even in the post-Mao era, describe how policy is made in the People's Republic of China. But it's a remarkably apt description of how big policy shifts occur in the United States of America.

If you prefer to take your political philosophy from an American, try John Gardner: "Very few—almost no—major policy innovations are enacted at the federal level that are not preceded by years (say, three to ten years) of national discussion and debate. The national dialogue is an untidy but impressive process. Ideas that will eventually become the basis for some major innovation in federal policy are first put into circulation by individuals and small groups."

It's hard to hold this model in our minds, because it turns on its head the traditional model of policymakers at the apex of a pyramid, experts and community leaders in the middle, and everyone else at the pyramid's wide bottom. But the task of leaders, as the experts in making something different happen, is to sniff out the sense of direction that is implicit in people's behavior, and then codify it, program it, and organize it—but not delude themselves that they invented or originated it.

I was struck at the time that, after President Reagan had been shot in 1981, U.S. Secretary of State Alexander Haig's announcement from the White House that "I am in control here" generated neither reassurance nor anger from the American people, but nervous laughter, as in watching theater of the absurd. We the people knew by instinct that, in a pluralistic democracy, no one is, can be, or is even supposed to be, "in control here." By constitutional design reinforced by the spread of knowledge, we live in a nobody-in-charge society.

Not long before that, in the late 1970s, I had tried systematically to record the major shifts in U.S. policy during the two preceding decades. I was testing a hunch that nearly all our nation's important changes in direction seemed to ooze out of the "governed," which would explain why the people formally entrusted with governing seemed nearly always to be playing catch-up. My conclusion was, and is, that major changes in society's sense of direction are first shaped in an inchoate consensus by the people at large.

Certainly the government was the last to learn that the war in Vietnam was over, or that Richard Nixon was politically dead.

American women had stopped having so many babies long before school boards and government planners adjusted to no-growth or slow-growth assumptions. Something similar happened when enterprises as varied as television studios and clothing man-ufacturers failed to realize that affluent seniors were becoming a much larger segment of the consumer market.

The rights of minorities, the status of women, and protections for the consumer would not have been where they already were then, if the people had waited for public executives or legislators— or university or business or religious leaders, for that matter—to take the initiative. The pressure boiled up from people (including new leaders) who had not previously been heard from.

Lots of people were opting for smaller cars long before Detroit caught on. The lag created a vacuum that Volkswagen, Honda, and Toyota were glad to fill.

On the ecological issues, the people seemed chronically to have been ahead of their leaders. They knew by instinct that air and water were no longer free goods, that energy was valuable and there-fore couldn't be cheap, that knowledge doesn't have to be applied just because it is known. A straw in that new wind had been the decision in the U.S. Senate not to go ahead with a commercial supersonic transport plane. Later the French and British govern-ments, after much expensive experience with the Concorde, wished they had come to that same early conclusion.

People-in-general got interested in energy conservation and sun-based forms of energy, and started worrying about global warming, while many leaders in energy policy, in government and in business, were still increasing U.S. dependence on Middle East oil, pooh-

poohing solar alternatives, driving around in gas-guzzling limousines, celebrating our huge coal reserves, and failing to practice rigorous energy conservation in their own organizations.

People-in-general were moving toward an ethic of qualitative growth while government and business leaders were still measuring growth by the grotesque yardstick called Gross National Product, which teaches that increases in food supply and in drug abuse are both indices of positive growth.

The American people also understood very early the dangers of betting heavily on nuclear power for electricity. Despite a strong pro-nuclear industry lobby with plenty of friends inside the Washington Beltway, they have resisted the building of new nuclear power plants in the United States for the past four decades.

The people also understood early, better and earlier than most defense experts, that big nuclear weapons are unusable except for deterrence of our peers. In quarrels with smaller powers, as Stanley Hoffman once put it, mere power can make us simply the biggest fly on the flypaper. (The Chinese have their own image: "Big Noise on Stairs Nobody Coming Down.")

As every surfer knows, it's not easy to catch a wave even when you know in what direction it is going—and impossible if you don't watch it very carefully. The task of leadership, then, is often to help the followers go where they already want to go—and if the leader gets too far behind, as President Nixon helped us all understand, he gets wiped out.

What seems to happen is that, if the policy question is important enough, people-in-general get to the answer first—because the information on which to make thoughtful judgments is readily available. The media serve as gatekeepers, moving information from its specialized sources to the general public, where it is then circulated through rapid-acting interpersonal networks, of which the most powerful and persuasive is still word of mouth. Then the experts and pundits and pollsters and labor leaders and lawyers and doctors and business executives, many of them afflicted with hardening of the categories, catch up in jerky arthritic moves with all deliberate speed.

And only then—when the policy decision has long since been made, and the experts have in consequence done the programming, written the editorials, raised the money, painted the directional signposts, and staged the appropriate media event—do the publicity heroes and heroines come forth. The people well-known for their well-knownness, the people that *People* magazine thinks are our leaders, climb aboard the train as it gathers momentum and announce for all to hear the new direction of march—speaking by television from the safety of the caboose.

It's more and more obvious: Those with visible responsibility for leadership are nearly always too visible to take the responsibility for change—until it becomes more dangerous to stand there than to move on. It's not a new idea: "I am a leader," Voltaire wrote, "therefore I must follow."

Education Is Revolution

The spread of education around the world has meant that change often starts with the students—especially those who take seriously the idea that the purpose of education is to enable them to think for themselves.

Once the students have pushed open a door (sometimes finding it surprisingly undefended), there are plenty of other people, and even some who regard themselves as leaders, who will gather to push it open further. These are often people with more years and experience, cowed into paralysis by that very experience, convinced at first that nothing can be done because it hasn't been done before, or protective of their small stake in not rocking the boat—until reckless young people such as those who at the end of 1989 stormed Nicolae Ceausescu's redoubt in Bucharest create a choice to be made, and long-suppressed frustrations move the more cautious folk to "vote with their feet" in choosing change.

The students still don't know how to manage an economy or govern a society, but they notice that their elders are not very good at management and governance either. What they *are* clear about is the need to open what has been closed, reveal what has been hidden, substitute human choice for subhuman fate, and draw all manner of untouchables from the periphery into the center where the choices seem to be made.

Many Americans have grown up thinking that American history offers a sort of map for the development of democracy. The United States celebrated, for thirteen years from 1976 to 1989, the two-hundredth anniversary of its nobody-in-charge experiment, the U.S. Constitution. But today's democracy movement is broader and deeper than the Declaration and Great Compromises conceived by that handful of bewigged and brilliant men, upper-class for their time, some of them still slaveholders, worldly, well-read men presuming to speak (with impressive clarity and eloquence) for people everywhere.

Now, women and men of all kinds and colors and modes of speech are sticking up for themselves, by the hundreds of thousands in one public square after another, by the millions when they get a chance to vote their own destiny. Their established leaders are behind them, way behind them, hurrying in breathless pretense that the new-style parades still need old-fashioned drum majors. Meanwhile, new leaders emerge, increasingly women as well as men, most of them educated people—journalists, writers, professors, labor leaders, entrepreneurs, civil servants—pushed into formal positions of power by the volcanic rumblings of the newly articulate crowds.

More Governance with Less Government

A tidal change of values is already well under way. The macrotask ahead of us is to manage a worldwide transition from indiscriminate and wasteful growth to purposeful, efficient, and compassionate growth. It includes enhancing the human environment with perceived energy and resource constraints, minimizing the damaging side effects of development, and guiding the growth of the presently richer societies to promote growth with equity in the presently poorer societies.

This task has to be undertaken in a world where no one race or creed or nation or alliance can, or should, arrogate to itself the function of general management: a pluralistic world society.

The main obstacle to converting these new values into policies, practices, and institutions is not limits to physical resources, or limits to the capacity of the human brain. It is the limits, even more recently discovered, to government.

If we are going to work out ways of governing ourselves without inflating our governments more and more, those with public responsibilities for public action are going to need continuous access to the best thinking of those who, because they are not publicly responsible, can more readily convert into suggested public policy the interest of the general public in getting the macrotask performed. And those of us who are privileged to think freely because we are not burdened with formal responsibility must be the first to widen our perspective and lengthen our view. Thus can non-officials partner with officialdom in the governance of a nobody-in-charge system.

The reactive mode of modern government ensures that most of the new ideas, especially about long-range goals and strategic paths toward them, originate outside government. The success of the Soviet Union in establishing for the government and the Communist Party a kind of monopoly of public-policy ideas and initiative turned out, in the end, to be a fatal self-inflicted weakness.

It was in the nature of communist governance that the political authorities—national governments and the communist parties that provided them with mass support and an ideological sense of direction—resisted the growth of grassroots civic organizations. They also brought into government itself those business and financial operations that seemed essential to the economy. And they did their best to co-opt and control the scientific academies, universities, and groupings of creative artists in which independent thinkers might threaten the power monopoly of the rulers and their central planners.

In 1995 the People's Republic of China hosted in Beijing a very large U.N. conference on the status of women. When it appeared that the official delegates would attract a large crowd of nonofficial women's organizations as well, the Chinese authorities moved the nongovernments to a remote location thirty miles from the intergovernmental meeting. Lincoln Bloomfield thus described the rationale for this extreme inconvenience: "Beijing's frantic efforts to isolate the parallel nongovernmental forum at [the U.N.] women's conference illustrated the need of tyrants to monopolize the process and keep any free-wheeling social element from slipping through the cracks."

Wherever communist governments were suddenly swept away, there was thus a large vacuum to be filled. In the politics of dissidence from communism, civil society (an Eastern European commentator wrote in the early nineties) meant "escape from public life . . . flight from the ubiquitous state into private forms of organization." Once free elections became the order of the day, the vacuum attracted a wide variety of new enterprise.

But enterprise needs to be reasonably fair to be reasonably free. As former dissidents came to power, a Romanian analyst told me, "the practice of power by those disgusted by it poses some serious issues." In the economic sphere, the initial absence of public regulation—and a flood of free-market advocacy from Western advisers who failed to explain the role of fair-market regulators in healthy Western economies—created a free-for-all in the newly freed markets of Central and Eastern Europe and democratic Russia.

Some criminal enterprisers, well-grounded in black marketeering, naturally took early advantage—and came to be called Mafia even if they had no connection with Sicilian-type conspiracies elsewhere. But so did many entrepreneurs anxious to make profits by providing people with goods and services they needed at prices they could afford to pay. And as governments, local as well as national, adjusted to the new environment, economic enterprise began to be free when it was constrained to be fair.

Where civil society plays an important role, politics is no longer just the struggle for governmental power. It encompasses an enormous range of systems for influencing decisions, making decisions, and carrying them into action. It includes the office politics of big organizations both private and public, the social-responsibility activities of corporations, the policy-relevant studies and statements of think tanks and university researchers, and the actions of thousands of nongovernmental organizations inside nations and among them.

The expanded role of civil society is consequently of growing importance in international relations. In the European Community, the complexity of nongovernment interactions has helped push European integration further and faster, by implicitly questioning the relevance of nation-states in ways no national political leader yet dared to explore out loud.

The extraordinary growth of global nongovernmental nobody-in-charge systems, ranging from currency exchange markets to the Internet, has created another arena in which governments and big corporations find they are unable to control either access or outcomes.

Both inside political states and among them, civil society is developing fast. In some ways and in many places, the networking among private people and organizations is already overmatching what is being done, what even can be done, by diplomacy among national governments. Inside countries and among them, civil society is clearly destined to be a major player in the wider politics of the twenty-first century.

In countries with thriving civil societies, an interesting division of labor results between nongovernmental experts, thinkers, and advocates on one hand, and government officials and legislators on the other. The nongovernments, it seems, can do some things better than governments can:

- They can work, ahead of time, on problems that are important but not yet urgent enough to command political attention.

- They can shake loose from conceptual confines and mix up disciplinary methodologies.

- They can think hard, write adventurously, and speak freely about alternative futures and what they suggest for public policy today.

- They can generate discussion among people in contending groups, different professional fields, and separate sectors of society who might not otherwise be talking to each other.

- They can organize dialogue across local, state, and national frontiers on issues not yet ripe for official negotiation.

I do not suggest that nongovernmental organizations are universally or even usually effective in compensating for the rigidities of responsibility. But the opportunity is always there. In the United States, it is reflected in the rapid growth of nongovernmental enterprise working under such rubrics as policy analysis, security studies, arms control, international economics, survey research (polling), environmental action, population research, public interest law, energy conservation, technology assessment—and *public affairs*, which can synthesize all of these into efforts to diagnose and prescribe for the situation-as-a-whole.

There is even a rough-and-ready test of relevance for nongovernment thinkers: are we working on issues that are still too vague, too big, too interdisciplinary, or too futuristic for governments that are too busy, too crisis-ridden, or too politically careful to tackle? If not, we should be.

So let's not neglect to include the nongovernments in a wider concept of governance. Maybe the key political dilemma, in this early part of the twenty-first century, can be expressed (like most truth) as an apparent paradox: How are we going to get more governance with less government?

The Malevolent Nongovernments

People-power is not always or necessarily beneficent. Criminals are people with power, too. The police power of governments has chronic difficulty catching up with criminal conspiracies that, because they operate internationally, are able to run drugs, launder money, and sometimes even topple weak national governments.

Interpol, the international club of national police forces, has developed an impressive system for exchanging information about criminals who don't respect the frontiers national governments think are so important. But the criminals' success in expanding the international drug trade suggests that their learning curve on information technology is also steep. As Anthony Judge of the Union of International Associations puts it, "Organized crime [is] still one neglected manifestation of 'civil society.'"

The most ambitious international terrorists have also been climbing a steep learning curve. Until recently the major terrorist threats came from semi-independent nongovernments, serving as government contractors—how else describe the relations between the hostage-taking Hezbollah in Lebanon and the government of Iran?

During the decade of the eighties, 6,500 international terrorist incidents occurred worldwide, leaving about 5,000 people dead and 11,500 wounded. Many of them had common features: the kidnapping or murder of innocent bystanders for purposes of extortion—whether the ransom sought was private money or public action such as the release of particular prisoners.

During the single morning of Tuesday, September 11, 2001, the terrorist attack on the United States broadened the identity, the definition, the scale, and the sophistication of terrorism.

Ramming hijacked airliners into both towers of New York City's World Trade Center and the Pentagon building near Washington (with other probable targets either aborted or planned for later on) was not the prelude to an extortionist's demand but a hate crime against a global range of targets—hated cultures, hated religious faiths, hatred for modernity itself (but with no reluctance to use its powerful technologies).

The attack targeted buildings that, whatever their symbolism, contained many thousands of people of every race and creed and color, and dozens of nationalities. More than three thousand people were killed; they could hardly be called anything but innocent bystanders. The purpose was plain and simple: to strike terror in multimillion hearts.

The "suicide bombers"—a suddenly inadequate description—
were clearly only a small part of an international conspiracy that
had the wit to fly in under the radar of the world's best intelligence
services by hiding in plain sight, communicating by conventional
e-mail, buying plane tickets over the Internet, using ordinary credit
cards and rental cars.

So gross an act against civilization will sustain a long-term, worldwide counterattack, as well as wholesale revision of thought about what
it takes to be secure in the new century. It should also focus newly
urgent attention about how people-power can prevent the use of the
dormant but dangerous products of modern science and technology,
including nuclear explosions, missile rocketry, the spreading of lethal
chemicals, and bioterrorism in both present and potential forms.

The more science-based future terrorist threats become, the more
the front-line defenses will have to be manned by civilians who are
closely following the sciences and technologies involved. In their
prescient 1990 report to the Swedish International Peace Research
Institute, Raymond Zilinskas and Carl-Göran Hedén described the
chilling prospect of genetic engineering being used to enhance lethal
toxins and increase the virulence of pathogens. Then they added:
"The probability of illicit activity being detected is low unless practitioners themselves are the ones who take the responsibility for
oversight. . . . The detailed practice of science is largely outside the
control of governments . . . it takes an expert to catch an expert."

The birthday of a new world is at hand. Building it, protecting
it, and making it safe for diversity—that's the personal responsibility we all find in the package marked "people-power."

Commentary on Chapter Five

Half a lifetime ago, I read an article by a valued academic colleague that seemed so far from what I knew and was learning about organizations that I just had to reply to it somehow. The article, in the *Saturday Review,* was titled "The Jungle of Hugeness," and was written by Kenneth Boulding, an economist whom I regarded as one of the great minds of the generation just before mine. It characterized large organizations with the metaphor of a brontosaurus and suggested, in effect, that the only way to deal with hugeness was to avoid it—rather than to understand it.

I was then dean of Syracuse University's Maxwell Graduate School of Citizenship and Public Affairs, the earliest (1924) and still, we thought, the best university-based effort to educate Americans for the public service. I had already worked in several very large U.S. government bureaucracies, and also in the huge postwar U.N. Relief and Rehabilitation Administration (UNRRA), managing its largest country program, in China. My experience of getting around in large organizations had been personally exciting and professionally rewarding, and I was just then teaching a graduate course about executive leadership, trying to convey to potential leaders how much fun they were going to have in their public service careers.

I was more than puzzled, I was somehow offended by Ken Boulding's metaphor about dinosaurs in a jungle of hugeness. So I called the *Saturday Review* and asked for equal time. The editors were delighted to host the debate; it's not only the practitioners of yellow journalism who see controversy as a spur to circulation.

What follows is my contrarian essay, edited and updated only enough to put most of it in the present tense—for this argument between smallness and bigness has lost none of its relevance in the first decade of the twenty-first century.

For the record, I still think that Kenneth Boulding was one of the brightest and also one of the most congenial colleagues I have ever been privileged to count as a friend.

5

Dinosaurs and Personal Freedom

Large-Scale Means *Loose*

It has become the fashion in recent decades to cry havoc about one particular example of social complexity—the weedlike growth of large-scale bureaucracies, public and private.

It is true, of course, that a finer division of labor and economies of scale encourage the erection of unwieldy-looking pyramids of authority. It is true that governments get bigger, corporations and labor unions get bigger, newspapers become fewer, and huge organizations make a growing proportion of the decisions that affect the welfare and destiny of us all. But is it true, as much of the literature on this subject would imply, that this trend puts our welfare and destiny in fewer and fewer hands? Does the individual have less choice or more?

My impression is that large-scale organization generally means loose organization—because if it isn't loose it doesn't work at all. Precisely because big organizations make most of the vital decisions affecting our destiny, many more people are participating in those decisions than ever before. The number of decisions that are important to our individual lives is multiplying so rapidly that it requires a growing proportion of the nation's population to serve as leaders in one context or another. The result of bigness is actually a diffusion of decision-making and decision-influencing ability far beyond the wildest dreams of Supreme Court Justice Louis Brandeis, who wanted to keep power diffused by keeping the units of society small.

In turn, the diffusion of power in so interdependent a society as ours means that each individual leader has more responsibility to fellow citizens than ever before. And so, as though in recompense for this added burden, American executive leaders find it possible to exercise more freedom of choice than ever before—*if* they learn how to operate within a large organization.

Case Against the Brontosaurus

In a 1958 *Saturday Review* article titled "The Jungle of Hugeness," Kenneth Boulding argued that things look bad for the individual in a world dominated by huge organizations, but cheerfully concluded there is a good deal of room in the interstices between the behemoths, where "individualists and people who positively like smallness of scale" can nevertheless survive. In the "Great Forest of society," a brontosaurus can do a lot of harm if it steps on you, but its feet don't take up much of the available acreage and there is plenty left over for the nimble and quick.

Throughout his article he seemed to assume that large organizations are single units, hierarchical, monolithic, and forbidding; that the only position of power in an organization was the number one spot; and that the interstices of freedom in our society were only *outside* large organizations.

None of these propositions tallied with my own experience.

Professor Boulding's alarm seemed to stem from the feeling that what he called the Organizational Revolution was tending to develop "ever greater degrees of hugeness."

> The electronic calculator, the punched card [remember he was writing in 1958], operations research, and decision theory all point to a still further revolution in the

making, to a still further removal of the scale barrier to the point, say, where General Motors (or the Pentagon, if by that time there is any distinction between the two) might absorb the whole American economy, and we would have, of course, a Communist State.

The case for capitalism is the case for smallness of scale . . . the case against the Brontosaurus—that beyond a certain point, increase in the scale of organization results in a breakdown of communication, in a lack of flexibility, in bureaucratic stagnation and insensitivity. There is a great deal of evidence to show that with present techniques of organization the scale barrier is reached long before we get to an organization the size of Soviet Russia, and that an attempt to organize a large economy as a one-firm state is doomed to inefficiency, corruption, and cruelty.

At first sight, even in America, things look bad for the individual.

Ken Boulding was a distinguished economist and I wasn't even an economist, so I had to assume that he had some evidence, not visible to my naked eyes, that persuaded him that the successes of American capitalism were due to smallness of scale. But his general picture depended for its logic on an even stranger notion: that the only countervailing power that might affect the behavior of General Motors, or for that matter the Soviet Union, was power *external* to those organizations. My observation, on the contrary, was that despite the tradition in business journalism to personalize corporations, very large organizations did not operate as single units with one commander in charge. Many, perhaps most, of their checks and balances were internal to the system. The tensions within the system were many—and so, therefore, were the opportunities for leadership.

Conditions of Freedom

In a household managed by people who can walk and talk (I argued then and still would today), a baby begins to experience a sense of personal freedom after mastering the arts of walking and talking. Just so, in an environment of large-scaleness, it is those people who learn to work with and in large-scale organizations who will have a rational basis for feeling free. There are, indeed, plenty of free men and women who work for giant corporations or government agencies—but they aren't those who scurry into the "interstices" of smallness.

What enabled the Soviet totalitarian system to survive for as long as it did may well be that a large number of middle-grade bureaucrats, and scientists and ballet dancers and other educated specialists, had so mastered the system that they were experiencing within its limits a significant measure of personal freedom. The Soviet Union was never a "one-firm state"; it was, rather, a myriad of organized groups of manageable size bound together not only by leaders proclaiming a manifest destiny but by millions of intricate personal relationships that glued things together in ways not so fundamentally different from other nations as they (and we) liked to assume. But of course the continuous effort to make the system run by top-down initiative deprived it of the enterprise and inventiveness of literally millions of its own citizens—which left it further and further behind the countries it regarded as its rivals.

My own occasional contacts with Soviet information technologies illustrated the growing gap. In one 1987 meeting at the Aspen Institute, a Soviet expert on education boasted that the U.S.S.R. would be placing half its next-year production of a million personal computers in its schools. Sitting around that table were corporate executives from, and academic specialists on, American information technology. We all knew that the U.S. was already producing several million PCs a year, and we had to keep from looking at each other to avoid laughing out loud.

Organizations do get bigger all the time. The Department of Defense, whose growth so alarmed Boulding, then employed 1,175,915 civilians in supervision and support of its soldiers, sailors, air force personnel, and Marines. It used nearly 10 percent of our gross national product. It was then spending more than the whole national product of Canada, Japan, India, or China, more than all the states and local governments in the United States, including public education for 40 million people from kindergarten through state universities.

Every other American institution was a dwarf by comparison with the Defense Department; my Maxwell School colleague Jay Westcott illustrated this proposition with a bagful of comparisons, circa 1958: Defense assets were greater than the combined wealth of America's hundred largest corporations (some of whose wealth, of course, came from large defense contracts). Some individual defense installations had a greater worth than the whole of the Ford Motor Company. The array of items purchased, distributed, and used for defense was forty times the size of that marketed by Sears Roebuck and Company.

Did facts such as these mean the Defense Department was a dangerously monolithic organization, that there were no freedoms in its civilian and military ranks, no interstices for individualists in the Pentagon building? Even then the President of the United States was having trouble organizing the Department's several satrapies under the effective control of a Secretary of Defense. That department has never been a unit. The larger it gets, the less likely it is to achieve effective unity. If it did come to be the monolithic structure Boulding seemed to fear, it would be dead on its feet. It is the internal tensions, reinforced by multiple cross-cutting external pressures, that keep it alive. In this respect at least, a body politic is not unlike the nervous system of a human being.

The Diffusion of Authority

"The bigger the organization," Ken Boulding wrote, "the smaller the proportion of its members who can really be at the top of the hierarchy and participate in the major decisions, and the larger the proportion who must carry out policies which are set higher up." But large organizations are just not like that. If anything, the dynamics work quite the other way around. A large and powerful organization has so many more important decisions to be made that there is proportionately more, not less, decision-making authority to be shared among a larger number of its members. The larger the organization and the wider its reach, the more lateral contacts have to be made within and outside it; thus, the more work there is for experts on complexity, which is to say *leaders*, whatever their nominal positions or ranks.

Moreover, in our society the larger the organization the more likely it is to be either a public agency or a private enterprise deeply affected with the public interest. In such an organization the number of major decisions about *internal* management may simply rise in arithmetic ratio to size. But the decisions about *external* relationships, the consent-building decisions that are in the broadest sense political, surely rise in something like geometric ratio.

In a large organization affected with the public interest (a category that includes nearly all large businesses and labor unions and nonprofits in our increasingly mixed economy), the nearer you get to the top of the so-called hierarchy the fewer unreviewed decisions you make.

The person who buys writing pads and pencils for a government agency makes lots of unreviewed decisions; if wrong decisions are made, they can be readily corrected in the next bulk procurement order or the next budget cycle. The President of the United States, by contrast, has to operate in a world peopled with countervailing organizations in and out of government that believe every presidential move is of concern to them, and should therefore be cleared with them. (Some of these are people who look as if they "work for" the President, if you were to judge from the organization chart.) The more countervailing organizations have to be consulted, the more members of the internal staff must be assigned to deal with them—and must therefore "participate in major decisions."

Finally, it is not true that in bigger organizations there is less room at the top. In Professor Boulding's time there may have been large companies with so little policy to be made that there was room for only one or two men who had the feeling they were participating in major decisions. But today, all large corporations are at least semi-public agencies; their heavy investments in lobbying Congress and state legislatures and penetrating executive regulatory agencies leave no doubt about how "affected with the public interest" they are. A government agency in its own jurisdiction wields such power that its seemingly lowly field representatives may legitimately feel involved in major decisions. Junior field inspectors of materiel for the Air Force may never get anywhere near the Secretary's office, but the inspectors' influence is great on matters they handle—and people judge themselves and are judged by others according to their influence (and their freedom of movement) within their own sphere.

My guess is that even in the Soviet Union there were lots of local Communist Party hacks who, though they never sat in on a meeting of the Presidium, had an equally solid basis for high morale. They fixed their attention on what made them big frogs in little ponds, and chose not to dwell on those aspects of their personal situation that would make them seem tiny frogs in the ocean of Soviet Communism. Closer to home: Despite an unimpressive position on the totem pole of the Federal bureaucracy, the county agricultural extension agent is a major player in local circles, disposing of substantial resources and representing, in the individual farmer's eyes, the power and weight of the U.S. government.

I have known field missions of the U.S. foreign aid program in which virtually every employee had a vivid sense of relevance in matters of importance to the country being helped—and to American foreign policy. The enterprise itself was palpably important, and the daily work of each person set precedents and could reinforce (or wreck) valued relations with a foreign country.

Ken Boulding concluded his provocative article by writing that "small organizations, even down to the level of the 'independent person,' will survive in the interstices between large-scale organizations." In modern interdependent society, with nearly all of us connected in multiple ways with each other, one does not easily find the referent for the term "independent person." But I suspect that those individuals will feel independent and self-confident who have learned how to survive and grow within large-scale organizations, not how to escape into the spaces between them. Perhaps Professor Boulding should have carried his image of the brontosaurus one step further: If my son Alan (our family's specialist on dinosaurs) is correctly informed, these huge beasts were remarkable for their surprisingly light tread.

Leaders All

It was a measure of the national mood that at the peak of American power we should be seized with the worry that large-scale organization is somehow a Bad Thing—that the very administrative skills that enabled us to build this strength and brought us free-world leadership is itself a threat to freedom.

My thesis here is the reverse: It is precisely by the development of administrative skills that we preserve and extend our freedom. The complexity of modern society and the omnipresence of large-scale organizations not only provide an opportunity for the fullest development of the responsible self; they actually place a premium on the exercise of a greater measure of personal responsibility by more people than ever before.

One of the results of modern technology and organization, for example, is to reduce the margin for error in a thousand ways. In the nineteenth century, most of the inhabitants of North America were scattered about on farms or in rural towns with plenty of room to spare. But now that three-quarters of us live in metropolitan and other urban areas, our accountability to each other is greatly enhanced.

Childhood activities that used to be tolerated in rural societies are now regarded in cities as "deviant behavior"; it is probably not so much high-spirited youth that has changed, but the norms of delinquency against which juvenile conduct is measured.

Similarly for adults, driving a Buick on a crowded speedway requires more continuous exercise of a sense of responsibility to others than driving a Model T on a rural byway. The pilot of a four-engine jetliner has to make more split-second decisions, and is responsible for more lives, than the driver juggling the reins of a stage coach.

Perhaps the most dramatic twentieth-century example was that of an air-defense team watching for enemy invasions through the Distant Early Warning line. As warning of attack became a matter of hours—and then of minutes—a heavy responsibility to all of us rested on the young men and women who interpret the electronic smears on their radar screens. Unleashing the U.S. capacity for massive retaliation against an enemy is a fearful responsibility, yet the demands of technology have not concentrated this decision but diffused it to the far corners of the earth where a sleepy GI could cost us precious time—or an overzealous one cost us much more than that.

In defense against less high-tech attack—the "suitcase bomb" of song and story, or the use of hijacked jet airliners as missiles in 2001—the heavy responsibility for prevention is spread among many thousands of inspectors at many hundreds of key airports, seaports of entry, and border crossings. Each of them knows how extremely unlikely it is that a dangerous terrorist has selected that place and this day to avoid detection. But for each of them to stay on the *qui vive* every day is a prime condition of our personal freedom.

In many less stirring but equally relevant ways, the complexity of society makes each of us vulnerable to the irresponsibility of others. If a man wanted to shoot up his neighbor in the Kentucky mountains, the other residents could avoid participation in the feud, which might smolder for generations as a "limited war" between two families. A similar feud cannot be tolerated in urban society. The interrelatedness of everything puts society's balance of power in the hands of the innocent bystander.

This increase in the extent to which each individual is personally responsible to others is most noticeable in a large bureaucracy. No one person decides anything; each decision of any importance is the product of an intricate process of brokerage among individuals inside and outside the organizations who feel some reason to be affected by the decision, or who have special knowledge to contribute to it. The more varied the constituency, the more the organization's decisions affect the public, the more outside veto-groups will need to be taken into account.

Even if no outside consultations are required, sheer size would produce a complex process of decision. For a large organization is a deliberately created web of tensions into which all individuals are expected to bring workways, viewpoints, and outside relationships markedly different from those of their colleagues. The task of the leaders, who will nearly always be plural, is to draw from these disparate forces the elements of wise action from day to day, consistent with the purposes of the organization as a whole.

Such a bureaucratic tension-system places a high premium on imagination, vigor, and qualities of personal leadership at all levels. The larger and more complex the organization, the more necessary it is for more of its members to learn and practice the art of building consent around a personal conviction—and reconciling it with the personal convictions of others. The finer the division of labor required, the more important it is for the scientist or economist or other specialist to understand the processes by which the expert's judgments are stirred into the administrative stew.

The expert is no longer just responsible for "presenting all the alternatives" in a thoughtful, scientific, scholarly manner. The expert must also figure out to whom to present them, and how, and what should be done and who should do it after one of the alternatives is selected. The expert is also responsible, in short, for being not only right but relevant—for getting the expert analysis understood by those who can't decipher the special language, for understanding the wider context that others in the game think they're dealing with, and for carrying outcomes to the point of action.

Thus in the world of large-scale organizations, everybody is now expected to understand—and practice in some degree—the arts of leadership. Those who take this obligation seriously will experience a sense of freedom—not in the interstices, but right in the middle of things.

Commentary on Chapter Six

"How can we be different together?" This deceptively simple question, asked by Magda Cordell McHale at a World Academy conference in Romania in the early nineties, sums up a prime dilemma of our time and suggests its own answer, too.

The failure to solve this puzzle peacefully has accounted for forty wars in the 1990s alone. Since the end of the cold war most of the many cultural, ethnic, and religious clashes have been rooted in unthinking assumptions that *different* and *together* cannot share the same sentence—or the same political boundaries.

The benefits of diversity have long been a subtheme in the education and upbringing of Americans. Yet our own history is overstuffed with examples of the limits we place on cultural diversity and of our discomforts with religious pluralism.

Now, in this new century, every American who reaches for leadership—who presumes to bring people together to make something different happen—will need to think hard about the complexity of "how to be different together" in our local communities and in our fractured world.

The framework of this essay derives from a 1995 article in *The Futurist* titled "The Limits to Cultural Diversity," parts of which derive in turn from some joint writing with Professor Lincoln P. Bloomfield in the mid-1980s. The comments on religion and governance are based on my collaboration with Marc Luyckx, who was then with the European Commission, on writings for the Brussels Seminar mentioned in the text. Yet another piece of this mosaic came from the World Academy's effort in the 1990s to make sense of the cultural, ethnic, and religious wars and refugee crises that have once again made "the Balkans" a metaphor for political instability.

6

"Safe for Diversity"

As the Eighties became the Nineties, the whole Sec-
ond World, as it used to be known, exploded and, in
a rather frenzied fashion, collapsed in upon itself. In
its place, a crater has suddenly opened up before the
eyes of an astonished world, one that is now spewing
forth a lava of post-communist surprises. Mixed up in
this lava, we will find a long-forgotten history coming
back to haunt us, a history full of thousands of eco-
nomic, social, ethical, ethnic, territorial, cultural,
and political problems that remained latent and unno-
ticed under the surface of totalitarian boredom.
—Vaclav Havel, February 1992

The Triple Collision

The cascade of European revolutions in 1989–1991 was part of a sea-
change featuring importunate crowds on four continents pushing
their leaders from behind and expressing a complex combination of
hopes and fears. Their hopes were hitched to spreading aspirations
about their human rights and rising expectations about their human
needs. But the hopes were mixed with fears—of discrimination,
exploitation, domination, conquest, or civil war—based on the
clash of cultural identities.

The wet blanket of the cold war had dampened both those hopes and those fears. It was much used to justify political oppression. It soaked up resources that might otherwise have been invested in education and economic development. It also squashed ethnic rivalries that interfered with spreading the dictatorship of the proletariat. The lifting of that wet blanket intensified the struggles for human rights and made possible a new war on poverty. But the new winds also blew into flame the smoldering embers of religious and cultural conflict.

It thus began to look as if three ideas we had thought were Good Things would be getting in each other's way: individual human rights, cultural human diversity, and global human opportunities. During the past decade, the damage from that triple collision has been all around us.

In 1994, in the middle of Africa, ethnicity took over as an exclusive value, resulting in the mass murder of more than a million Rwandans by butchery, spreading from Rwanda into the Congo, drawing into the Congo's "internal affairs" national armies of five neighboring countries—Uganda and Rwanda, Angola and Zambia and Zimbabwe.

In ex-Yugoslavia, gunpowder and rape soon began to serve the same ugly purpose—trampling on human rights and erasing human opportunities in the name of ethnic cleanliness.

Even on the Internet, where individuals can now join global groups not defined by place-names or cordoned off by gender or ethnicity, people are choosing sides on cultural issues and shouting at each other in flaming, capital-letters rhetoric.

Look hard at your home town, at the nearest inner city; scan the world by radio, TV, or newspapers and magazines. What has happened is all too clear: Just when individual human rights have achieved superstar status in political philosophy, just when information technology promises what the U.N. Charter calls "better standards of life in larger freedom," culture and diversity have formed a big, ugly boulder in the road called Future.

"If we cannot end now our differences, at least we can help make the world safe for diversity." That was the key sentence in the most

influential speech of John F. Kennedy's presidency: his commencement address at American University on June 10, 1963. That speech led directly, among other things, to the first nuclear test ban treaty.

For nearly three decades more after that, we were mesmerized by the threat of strategic nuclear war. But now, a big nuclear exchange has clearly become the least likely eventuality among the major threats to human civilization. And that brings us face to face with the puzzle identified in Kennedy's speech: how to make diversity safe.

The Fear of Outsiders

Is "cultural diversity" really the new Satan in our firmament? Or does it just seem so because *culture* is being used—as *Kultur* has been used in other times and places—as an instrument of repression, exclusion, and extinction?

In today's disordered world, the collision of cultures with global trends is in evidence everywhere. Ethnic nations, fragmented faiths, transnational business, and professional groups find both their inward loyalties and their international contacts leading them to question the political structures by which the world is still, if tenuously, organized.

During the 1990s, more of the world's people seemed to move each year than moved the year before—each year, more than ever before in world history—driven by fear of guns and machetes or yearning for more food and greater freedom. This mobile world has induced many millions of people to believe that their best haven of certainty and security would be a group based on ethnic similarity, common faith, economic interest, political like-mindedness, or some combination of these.

Societies based on fear of outsiders tend toward totalitarian governance. Fear pushes the culture beyond normal limits on individuals' behavior. "To say that you're ready to *die* for cultural identity," said a colleague at a 1994 workshop of the World Academy of Art and Science in Romania, "means that you're also ready to *kill* for cultural identity." Said another: "The ultimate consequence of what's called 'cultural identity' is Hutus and Tutsis murdering each other."

The fear that drives people to cleave to their primordial loyalties makes it harder for them to learn to be tolerant of others who may be guided by different faiths and loyalties. But isolating oneself by clinging to one's tribe is far from a stable condition. These days, tribal solidarity is itself highly unstable, as many fierce local wars in Africa bear witness. Even without threats from armed incursions, differences in birth rates and ecological pressures to move will continue to mix populations together. So ethnic purity isn't going to happen, even by forcible "cleansing."

Besides, cultures keep redefining themselves by mixing with other cultures, getting to know people who look, act, and believe differently. In today's electronic world, cultures are routinely exposed to new faiths and fashions, new lifestyles, workways, technologies, clothing, and cuisines.

The Outbreak of Diversity

TV viewers in the West watched in awe (mixed with some euphoria) the breakup of the great ice-floes of the cold war. Some of the large icebergs thus freed to float in the warmer waters of world politics have now in their turn broken up into smaller icebergs. Separatist ambitions are especially eruptive when they are combined—as they now are in most societies—with resentments and reactions in the name of cultural identity and religious tradition. The result, in many parts of the world, has turned out to be more dangerous to peace and security than the frozen antagonism of the two nuclear superpowers used to seem.

What is most striking about the revolutions of the late twentieth century is not, after all, the cascade of conversions to democracy. It is the outbreak of cultural diversity—the boiling over of resentments in the name of almost forgotten or newly discovered cultural traditions.

Sociologist Elise Boulding wrote some years ago about "the 10,000 societies living inside 168 nation states." Even that arresting way of putting it understated a complexity in which so many of the "10,000 societies" are transnational, in no sense "inside" the familiar political lines on conventional world maps.

There are multimillions of overseas Chinese. Millions of disgruntled Russians crowd the new republics bordering Russia. And there are millions of Hungarians and Romanians and Turks in other peoples' countries, millions of Muslims and Hindus and Sikhs living in each other's laps in the Asian subcontinent, millions of Catalans and Basques and Kurds and Palestinians and Tamils and Ibos and Zulus and Tibetans, millions of Québecois and North American Indians, who don't acknowledge as their "nation" the "state" in which they find themselves.

All of Africa will need to find new dimensions of racial tolerance and racial sharing. Japan cannot be both a world power and an island of racial purity. India's future governance will have to feature a large measure of uncentralized politics—else what is now India, already chopped into three parts since independence from the British, could turn out to be several more countries.

With Western Europe moving toward integration, the breakup of Yugoslavia heralded the Balkanization of the Balkans. A friend in Paris estimates that there are more practicing Muslims than practicing Catholics in France—a slippery statistic that depends too much on what *practicing* means but nonetheless signals a major change in recent decades. Islam is also the fastest-growing organized religion in the United States. Mass migrations and differential rates of procreation are creating more and more societies where "everybody's a minority."

That has long been the basis for Hawaii's hothouse ethnic politics. It is in California's horoscope, too—already reality on its university's Berkeley campus. Before long, "everybody's a minority" may be the story of political demography in a couple of dozen U.S. states. This does not, by the way, mean that the metaphor of the "melting pot" is finally coming true in America. The durably distinctive cultures of immigrants from elsewhere—Anglo-Saxons, Africans, Scandinavians, Irish, Germans, Italians, Poles, Jews and Arabs from many countries, Mexicans, Central and South Americans, Chinese, Koreans, Japanese, Southeast Asians, Indians, Pakistanis, Iranians,

Afghans, and so many others, along with the rapidly growing number of citizens (such as golfer Tiger Woods) who call themselves "multiracial"—are all part of "American culture."

The idea of a multiracial, multicultural society with both a national gist and a global perspective, pioneered in fits and starts by the United States, Canada, and Brazil, may prove to be one of the enduring social innovations of the twentieth century. But Indonesia's late-twentieth-century history showed how fragile and precarious such unity-with-diversity can be.

Information Technologies and Cultural Identity

What is "cultural identity?"

Artist and futurist Magda McHale (Hungarian by birth, educated in Slovakia, living with a British passport in Buffalo, New York) argues that in the modernized world—even in those societies that overtly resist modernization—nobody's cultural identity remains untouched by external influences.

The identity of each of us is "like a collage, made up from fragments of different images, old and new, juxtaposed—creating a wholly new 'picture' that is well-balanced and pleasing," at least to ourselves. Each of us is "a slowly changing kaleidoscope of identities in a changing landscape of influences and circumstances. . . . Human beings constantly reshape their memories about their past, rearrange and reselect events and impressions to fit their present expediencies."

The past is only prologue, not a forecast. According to this analysis, no "group culture" is more than partly valid; some are largely fictional.

In imagining ourselves we combine the old—deep instincts and inherited ideas—with the new, which often means genuinely new in that it was never before scientifically conceivable or technologically possible. The threat to robust cultures (those that can meld the best of the new with the best of the old) comes from both extremes: an unthinking attachment to what has already been thought or done, and an overenthusiastic espousal of what is new because it is new.

Modern information technologies seem, on the whole, to promote cultural diversity. Some observers feel that a worldwide culture is developing. They point to the sameness around the world of blue jeans, soft drinks, fast food, TV programs, and attack weapons. I am equally impressed with the growing diversity: McDonald's hamburgers and Kentucky Fried Chicken coexist in every world city with an expanding variety of ethnic and regional cuisines—French, Italian, Greek, Chinese, Japanese, Indian, Mexican, Thai, Vietnamese, and many others.

Even what is now universally called "rap" (in Paris, *le rap*), which *Time* magazine called "possibly the most successful U.S. export this side of the microchip," seems to have developed an infinite cultural variety. Rap is, to be sure, often a medium of ideological protest, but the targets are likely to be nearby wrongs. "We express the same message," an Italian rap artist tells an Italian magazine, "the disease of Italian society."

The world's most information-intensive societies, which happen by no coincidence to be the postindustrial democracies, are (with one obvious Japanese exception) the most heterogeneous and fragmented in their cultural patterns. Information technologies, especially those such as the telephone, cable and satellite TV, and personal computers that enlarge the range of individual human choice (with whom to converse, what to watch, how and where to work), continuously expand the range of individual options and increase the complexity of the "collage."

It is true that cultural tradition is often a drag on social change. This is true not only of antique customs, rituals, myths, and mores, but also of narrow "modern" cultural mindsets (some scientists' concepts of "proof," some economists' notions of "equilibrium," some artists' dedication to circles or cubes) that are not much help in the situation-as-a-whole integration that is the essence of leadership for change.

But where information technologies—computers, satellites, and telecommunications fused in working systems—are especially influential is in creating, for millions of people at a time, a common awareness of needs for behavioral change—for example, to protect public health and the global environment—and common norms such as the idea of inherent human rights.

Information technologies have also made it much easier to maintain communication among the like-minded, regardless of geography. Global assertions of community, as in the Jewish diaspora and the Roman Catholic Church, are no longer rare; they are matched now by uncounted transnational advocacy groups and terrorist conspiracies. Even leaders of cultural movements that take an anti-modern stance, such as the Shi'ite clerics of Iran, do not hesitate to use computers and audiocassettes to rally the faithful at home, and co-opt the TV news services to press their claims for ransom and recognition abroad.

So, far from melding the world's rich diversity of cultures into an undifferentiated lump, the global technologies that show the world as one also help intensify a whirlwind of conflict among tribes, ethnic groups, belief systems, and "nations" in the original, cultural sense of that word. André Malraux, the author who became France's Minister of Culture, was no neophyte on global impacts of information technology. Yet before he died near the end of the twentieth century, he made a prediction worth pondering: "The twenty-first century is going to be the century of religion."

Diversity Within Religions

If Malraux guessed right, what kinds of conflict are likely to occur in the century just begun? The easy answer is that the Great Religions will collide in the historic "clash of civilizations" envisaged in the recent writings of Samuel Huntington.

The gigantic assault of September 11, 2001, on the World Trade Center and the Pentagon may even have been planned with the idea that it would provoke "the West" into so broad a retaliation against "the Muslim world" as to generate just that kind of global clash.

In 1998 the European Union was puzzling about religious diversity as part of its effort to think through its coming *European* foreign policy. I was then president of the World Academy of Art and Science; the European Commission asked us to help organize a "Brussels Seminar on Civilisations and Governance," bringing in from other parts of the world scholars who could interpret current trends in all the world's great religions. In preparation for that event, I collaborated with Mark Luyckx, a creative futurist on the commission staff, in drafting a concept paper on religions and governance to frame the issues for discussion.

As we saw it, the "clash" that is really making its way to center stage in world politics is the split within each religious tradition between so-called fundamentalists on one hand and the modernists they fear on the other. But there is an emerging worldview we called "transmodern" that also calls into question the modern worldview—but for very different reasons.

The fundamentalists of many faiths—in Eric Hoffer's language, "true believers"—feel threatened by modern society. They resent everything from its outlandish music to its overwhelming technologies to its overbearing assumption that those who aren't modern are backward, underdeveloped, and imprisoned by tradition. They see their traditional scriptures and teachings as absolute, dividing humankind into irreconcilable believers and infidels.

What we called "transmoderns" are more inclined to see their ancient traditions or new spiritual insights as raw material for wider human reconciliation, as the basis for an intensified search for common purposes among people of diverse races, creeds, and national origins. The emerging vision is a world safe for religious diversity. The image might be represented by a round table, around which people of both genders and all races, cultures, and faiths consider and negotiate about how to manage our common planetary home—in ways responsible not only to its current inhabitants but to their grandchildren's grandchildren as well.

There is plenty of room in this pluralistic scene for striving toward an ultimate, universal Truth. But the search requires tolerance of other peoples' paths to the elusive goal, and tolerance also of the differing liturgies with which they celebrate the goal and describe their search. And it doesn't require any seeker to concede that any of the other seekers has already found the Holy Grail—or that the universal or pluralistic search can therefore be called off.

"The goal," as John Gardner has written about communities large and small, "is to achieve wholeness incorporating diversity. That is the transcendental task for our generation."

The pedestal of Reason, the icon of modernity, was in the twentieth century eroded by the experience that science and technology can lead not only to miracles of constructive change but also to rationally planned troubles. New kinds of science, such as chaos theory, seem to depend as much on intuition as on reasoning; some scientists are talking about how much they don't know and can only pray to understand. And what once seemed the rational ways to organize human cooperation—hierarchies, pyramids, bureaucracies—are increasingly in disrepute.

As Max Weber explained long ago, modernity was bound to disenchant the world. The meaning of our individual and collective lives was radically secularized; life and death were explained as rational processes; our hearts were separated from our brains, our souls detached from both.

Now a new way of thinking presents itself as a genuine option: the healing notion that body, mind, and spirit are integrated parts of a human whole; that a logic different from modernity is not only conceivable but attractive; that sacred texts, present-day spiritual insights, and rational science are all valid sources of a transmodern philosophy.

What's emerging, then, is a mindset that tolerates, even celebrates, diversity. It embraces the openness that modern information technologies make possible, even necessary. It includes the dawning realization that scientific discovery and technological innovation have made human beings the dominant actors in their own future evolution. It is open to spiritual guidance as relevant to both private behavior and public policy. And it moves away from vertical authority systems toward more networked organizations, more consensual decision making.

This mindset, we suggested, "has implications for religions and their impact on governance in the early part of the twenty-first century." One is that "organized religions will be sharing their turf with 'unorganized spirituality.'" Episcopal Bishop Swing of San Francisco forecast "an increasing number of 'spiritual refugees' looking where to invest their souls," and deplored "the squandering of the treasure chest of spirituality which [organized] religions could offer the world if they could grow beyond mutual hatred to a place of mutual respect."

Another implication of the transmodern mindset is that the leadership of organized religion, "traditionally monopolized by men, will increasingly be shared by women." Yet another is "that the acceptance of variety, the protection of diversity, and doctrines of tolerance seem more and more essential to security and survival." A fourth is "an increasingly global perspective."

Because it leaves room for traditional sources of inspiration, the transmodern way of thinking may be the most valid alternative to the rigidity of fundamentalists in every religious tradition, and provide also an escape from the secular intolerance of spiritual insight.

The most striking outcome of the EU's Brussels Seminar was that our description of an emerging transmodern mindset elicited very positive response from the nonwestern scholars.

A Buddhist scholar, Susantha Goonatilake, foresaw the center of economic gravity moving toward Asia, and a return to "our cultural and religious roots in order to bring . . . our specific cultural richness and wisdom [to] the future management of a more sustainable and just world." "The Confucian way to identify ourselves is through family," said Kim Tae-Chang. With this broad family concept, Confucian culture can "transcend the boundaries of egoism and push toward solidarity with the actual and future generations."

Asked to analyze Muslim reactions, Ziauddin Sardar (currently editor of the British journal *Futures*) said that Islam is "working modernity out of our system. . . . Change has to be accommodated, but the fundamental tenets of tradition, the source of [Islam's] identity and sacredness, remain the same. So we may define a transmodern future as a synthesis between life-enhancing tradition—that is amenable to change and transition—and a new form of modernity that respects the values and lifestyles of traditional cultures."

"The West has always seen Islam through the lens of modernity," he added, "and concluded that it is a negative, closed system. Nothing could be farther from the truth. Islam is a dynamic, open system with a very large common ground with the West. . . . Islam is intrinsically pluralistic. It considers that in essence every culture has a piece of the truth."

The implication was clear: Islam is rejecting, not the West, but some aspects of modernity. The transmodern way of thinking might open a door to a new Western dialogue with mainstream Islam—though not with a terrorist fringe that seeks destruction rather than dialogue.

Cultural Diversity on Collision Course

Cultural and religious diversity are troublesome to majority elites and authorities, who tend to respond to separatist ambitions with discrimination, suppression, even extermination. Diversity is also enormously valuable; it's what the world needs to be made safe for. But it's now on collision course with two other values on which the twenty-first century will also have to be built.

One of these collisions is the clash of "group rights" asserted by ambitious cultural, racial, and even religious communities with the contrasting ideology of "human rights," individual and inalienable—the idea that a person has rights not by virtue of belonging to a nation, a religion, a gender, a class, an ethnic category, or even a family, but by virtue of having been born into the human race.

The other collision with diversity comes from the "outward push" of modern science and technology, which makes it possible to think of the world as one—as a global market for goods and services and money, as an integrated biosphere to be monitored and protected, as a global community in which nuclear war and human hunger might be outlawed.

The strong desire to cleave to a "we," against an unfamiliar and presumably hostile "they," is among the most basic of human instincts. In world politics this urge creates many communities—bonded by ethnicity, religion, and ideology—whose "inward pull" is in tension with the imperatives and promises of science and technology.

These require the coalescence of wider communities to handle functions that cannot be tackled alone by even the most powerful nations or global corporations—functions symbolized by the U.N.'s peacemaking mediators and peacekeeping forces, the World Weather Watch, the care and safety of refugees, the control of infectious diseases, safety systems for civil aviation, cooperation in agricultural research, the environmental cleanup of regional seas, and the management of the global commons (the oceans, the atmosphere, outer space, and Antarctica).

At every political level the willingness of leaders to coordinate their problem-solving efforts with "foreigners" is constrained by the inherent, centripetal pull of sociocultural roots. The tug of belongingness is what glues together every power structure from family to empire; people cherish their own ways and want to retain whatever freedom of action they can. "Politics gives people something, and somebody, to believe in," says Professor Yehezkel Dror of the Hebrew University in Jerusalem. "There's a desire for solidarity, and dangers in solidarity. The leader's task is to be able to tell the difference."

People feel empowered by banding together with those they know against those they do not know. This is, indeed, the way people preserve their sense of individual worth when faced with the uncertainties of nature and the impersonality of big institutions and big ideas—corporations, governments, religious doctrines, economic theories, or abstractions such as "world order." This is why each cooperative move outward from village, neighborhood, nation, or state is in tension with the natural inward pull of community. The burden of proof is always with those who propose to coordinate the in-group's policies and practices with outsiders.

The pull of community is equally in evidence in communities that are joined not by geography but by other bonds such as race ("the white man's burden"), religion (universal faiths, missionary societies), professional solidarity (Olympic athletes, the international community of scientists), or common economic interest such as transnational corporations or OPEC, the Organization of Petroleum Exporting Countries.

It is tempting for theorists of world order to see these transnational communities (or at least the ones they approve of) as networks that undermine, and might in time supplant, the geography-based sovereignty of the national state. But communities of religion, language, consanguinity, specialization, or like-mindedness are hardly likely to be less narrow in their outlook, less prone to analyze their interests in we/they terms, than villages or principalities or nation-states that have had to bury a good many local hatchets in order to achieve any sense of community at all.

"Global village" is thus an oxymoron, not the most creative way to think about a boundary-transcending system of peaceful change for the next historic period. But neither is reconstruction of the system likely to come from the fragmentary worldviews of nuclear physicists, resource oligopolists, plant physiologists, religious fanatics, or stars of track and field.

In sum: the centripetal pull of community, which gives us all part of our valued identities, is an important component of reality. So also is the value of each person as an individual. So also is the need to shape more inclusive communities and institutions made possible by modern knowledge. What's unique cannot be universal. What's universal threatens, and is threatened by, what's unique.

Therefore, while celebrating cultural diversity and the political change it's bringing about on every continent, we need to think hard about reconciling it with both individual human rights and global human opportunities.

Culture Shock

In the aftermath of the Rwanda bloodbath, while the internecine warfare in Bosnia was gathering momentum, the World Academy of Art and Science helped bring together in Europe a group to think hard about what cultural clashes were doing to "Western civilization," which most of us had (at least recently) considered rather stable and nonexplosive. This peaceful seminar was held while several wars rooted in ethnic, religious, and cultural rivalries were under way or heating up in Southeastern Europe.

The early stage of every realization of cultural identity, every assertion of a newfound right to be different, does create a distinct group marked by ethnic aspect (black is beautiful), gender (women's movement), religion (chosen people), or status as a political minority (Hispanics in U.S. politics). But when members of a group insisting on the group's uniqueness do succeed in establishing their own personal right to be different, something very important happens: They begin to be treated *individually* as equals; the incidence of intermarriage increases; and they tend to integrate, at least in superficial ways, with the more inclusive communities.

Before the fighting in Yugoslavia, the most tolerant people in that part of the world were seen by their close neighbors to be the Serbs, Croats, and Muslims living together in Bosnia-Herzegovina, with the city of Sarajevo regarded—it was hard to believe in the 1990s—as a special haven of mutual tolerance, even love.

The problem does not seem to be cultural differences, but cultural overenthusiasm. Cultural loyalties, said a world-class Croatian physicist, have the makings of a runaway nuclear reaction. Without the moderating influence of civil society—acting like fuel rods in a nuclear reactor—the explosive potential gets out of hand. What's needed is the counterforce of wider views, global perspectives, more universal ideas.

Postcommunist societies, said a resident of one of them, have experienced a loss of equilibrium, a culture shock from the clash of traditional cultures, nostalgia for the stability of Soviet culture, and many new influences from outside. What's needed, he thought, is cultural richness without cultural dominance, but with the moderating effect of intercultural respect.

Civilization and Culture

The World Academy colleagues felt we had all inherited a fuzzy vocabulary that sometimes treats *culture* as a synonym for *civilization*. We experimented with an alternative construct:

Civilization is what's universal—values, ideas, and practices that are in general currency everywhere, either because they are viewed as objectively true or because they are accepted pragmatically as useful in the existing circumstances. These widely accepted truths offer the promise of weaving together a *civitas* of universal laws and rules, becoming the basis for a global civil society.

What is sometimes called *management culture* appears to be achieving this kind of universal acceptance, hence becoming part of global civilization. Nobody has to be in charge of practices that are generally accepted.

The international exchange of money—a miracle of information technologies—is remarkably efficient, every week moving trillions of dollars' worth of money among countries. Quite literally no one is in charge of the system that makes this happen. There are some technical standards worked out in agreement among central banks, to make sure that everyone using the system understands its vocabulary and knows how to use its information technologies. But no central authority is giving orders, depriving outsiders of access or cutting insiders in on its benefits. Indeed, the puny efforts of governments to control monetary swings by buying and selling national currencies have only demonstrated governments' incapacity to control them.

If civilization is what's universal, *culture* is the substance and symbols of community. Culture meets the basic human need for a sense of belonging, for participating in prides and fears shared with an in-group.

Both culture and civilization are subject to continuous change. In our time, the most pervasive changes seem to come with the spread of knowledge, the fallout of information science and information technologies.

Civil society consists of many structures and networks that cut across cultural fault lines and are brought into being by their ability to help people communicate. Some are not very dependent on public authority for their charters or their funding, and even mount advocacy efforts to influence public policy. Others are deliberately brought into being by public authorities to take on functions (such as low-income housing projects and welfare programs) that used to be considered the responsibility of national governments.

Many of these "nongovernments"—such as those concerned with business and finance, scientific inquiry, the status of women, population policy, the global environmental commons, and the protection of cultural diversity itself—have become effective users of modern information technologies. In consequence, they are providing more and more of the policy initiative both inside countries and in world affairs.

Civilization is rooted in compromise—between democracy and authority, between a free-market economy and a caring economy, between openness and secrecy, between vertical and horizontal relationships, between active and passive citizenship. The required solvent for civilization is respect for differences. The art is *to be different together.*

Civilization will be built by cooperation and compassion, in a social climate in which people of different groups can deal with each other in ways that respect their cultural differences. "Wholeness incorporating diversity" was philosopher John Gardner's succinct formulation. The legend on U.S. currency is even shorter, perhaps because it's in Latin: *E pluribus unum* ("from many, one"). Helping the many think of themselves as one, selling wholeness that can incorporate diversity, will be a central challenge for many different kinds of leaders in the twenty-first century.

Commentary on Chapter Seven

I will freely admit that I wasn't trained as a scientist—and even as what's called a political scientist, I have long felt that politics is more art than science. But I have had a lifelong fascination with the impacts of science on society, and many of the jobs I've held have fed and enhanced that fascination.

In April 2000 I was invited to lecture at Blinn College, not far from Texas A&M, in a series exploring the mysteries of biotechnology and genetic engineering. I thought it might be fun to try to capture and record a way of thinking that, while implicit in much of what I have done, had never been pulled together in one writing.

Most of this essay is derived from that lecture. I have added the story about the World Weather Watch, to illustrate my hope and conviction that leaders who are not scientists don't always have to be playing catch-up with scientific discovery and technological innovation.

7

The Social Fallout of Science

Biologists Having a Ball

Forty-seven years ago, in company with journalist-historian Theodore H. White, I spent an evening with Victor Weisskopf, one of the physicists who had worked on the world's first nuclear weapons. But what I remember most vividly is not what he said about physics or the Bomb.

As we wound up our interview I asked him whether, if he were to start all over again, he would be a physicist. "No, I'd want to be a biologist," he replied without hesitation. After a pause, his face broke into a smile of pure delight. "What a wonderful field! They don't know anything yet. They don't know what life is. They don't know what goes on inside a cell."

The life scientists still don't claim to know just what life is, or why; they can't even agree when it starts. But they *are* learning what goes on inside a cell, and even how to change the lively behavior of its tiny components.

Nature and nurture, which used to be separately taught and studied, have come together in molecular biology. Genetic engineers are learning how to move genes in and out of species. Computer experts are stretching the limits of speed and memory to map the whole of the human genome. Scientists have married genetics and chemistry to begin to decipher our most powerful information

93

system, the one we are born with. As Weisskopf predicted, the biologists and their friends are having a ball.

And in the new branch of engineering called biotechnology, they are developing know-how that will enable us—human beings, *homo* we hope *sapiens*—to mastermind our own evolution. So the citizens who reach for leadership in the twenty-first century take on more responsibility for our destiny than leaders in any other times and places.

Before speculating on the social consequences and policy implications of the life sciences, I have two stories to tell. One is a cautionary tale, sketching three centuries of history that teach us to be careful about remaking ourselves through science and technology. The other is a story from personal experience, suggesting that it *is* possible for students of society and builders of institutions to work in parallel with the sci-tech discoverers and innovators in every field—if we don't wait to be prodded into action by front-page drama and disaster.

A Newtonian Mold

Think back three centuries. The bold political thinking that led to the U.S. Constitution 215 years ago was rooted in an even bolder leap of the human imagination just a hundred years before.

In 1687 Isaac Newton, standing on the shoulders of Copernicus and Kepler, proposed a force of universal gravitation to explain why the planets revolved around the sun in elliptical paths. This force, he figured, loses effect with the square of the distance. That same force, he also guessed, keeps the Moon in motion around the Earth, keeps our feet on the ground, and causes objects (such as Newton's famous apple) to fall to Earth. It's still a pretty good guess.

But Newton couldn't imagine that the Scientific Revolution he helped start would in time become a kind of secular religion, the scientific method binding together an influential new international priesthood.

He certainly didn't foresee that in a very few centuries, people might generate the knowledge and acquire the capacity to do more to their natural environment than nature does to, and for, people. Yet this is where we are today. An ironic anonymous couplet says it all:

Strange that man should make up lists of living things in danger.
Why he fails to list himself is really even stranger.

We got into this fix because our thinking about society—about economics, about politics, even about philosophy and religion—was mesmerized by the success story of what we called natural science.

It was not until Newton had pictured the universe as guided by precise laws of motion, tending to harmonize the forces of nature, that John Locke found in the "laws of nature" the foundation for human society, Adam Smith discovered an "invisible hand" to guide trade and industry according to the (natural) law of supply and demand, and James Madison suggested that a balance among "factions" might, like the counterpoise of heavenly bodies, provide a democracy with built-in self-control.

Eighty years after the United States was born in this Newtonian mold, Charles Darwin's theory of natural selection made room for a nastier mode of social thinking: unpremeditated struggle, wasteful and chaotic, replaced order and reason as the central dynamic.

The already rich and powerful soon found in Darwin's idea an argument against compassion, a justification for cruelty and selfishness: If you were poor, that just proved that you were unfit. (The theme still reverberates in debates about welfare policy.)

After another half-century, along came Albert Einstein with his intuition that matter and energy are aspects of each other, and his search for a general theory of relativity. The notion that "everything is relative" soon became a powerful new social metaphor, popularizing the behavioral approach to social science and further eroding religions that depended for their clout on moral discipline and unquestioning faith.

It became quite respectable to believe that eternal verities might well be proven wrong by further study—the students meanwhile suspending judgment on whatever they might have learned at home, in church, or at school. The Pope, visiting the United States in 1987, encountered science-based skepticism at every whistle-stop.

Beginning in the 1960s, yet another new social outlook emerged from the profound discoveries of the life sciences (the cracking of the genetic code, the glimmerings of what goes on inside a cell), and growing scientific interest in the linkage of biology, chemistry, physics, meteorology, economics, and geophysics to decipher food-climate-population-energy puzzles.

Quite suddenly, the evidence seemed overwhelming that everything really is somehow related to everything else. Ecology and environmental protection came into vogue. The key word—parallel to *harmony*, *struggle*, and *relativity* in the earlier cosmologies—was *interdependence*.

A New Kind of Reformation

The buoyant optimism of Newton's harmonious equations is deeply embedded in the logic of modern science. The march of science and technology, in this view, is as beneficent as it is inevitable.

I suppose that's why the Manhattan Project, the huge secret wartime enterprise that produced the first two atom bombs, did not employ on its ample staff a single person whose full-time assignment was to think hard about the consequences if the project should succeed. No one was working on nuclear arms control—and we've been playing catch-up ever since.

When I was ambassador to NATO in the late 1960s, I mentioned this curious lapse in a talk to the NATO Science Committee. The committee chairman was Dr. I. I. Rabi, Nobel laureate in physics at Columbia University and an old friend of mine; he had worked closely with Robert Oppenheimer, who managed the Manhattan Project. "Harlan, you shouldn't say things like that," Dr. Rabi complained. "Oppie and I used to discuss nuclear arms control all the time." Observing my skeptical reaction, he added two words: "—at lunch."

Nowadays, the mood is different. Science-and-technology has produced so much dirt and smog and ugliness, so many explosions and crashes in fail-safe systems, so much wasted weaponry and undisposable waste, that popular resistance to the inner logic of the scientific method grows louder every year.

The one thing we cannot do, in our information-rich environment, is to keep people quiet about all this. Several billion people now know or suspect that science has created the capacity to end it all—or, in the alternative, to make the human adventure wonderfully endless. The spread of mass education, speeded and supplemented by the Internet, has brought in its train a widespread demand for wide participation to make sure the policy decisions about the wonders and the dangers of modern science are widely shared.

Three centuries after Newton, we the people seem determined to take science and technology off automatic pilot and steer them toward the fulfillment of human aspirations—beginning with what Samuel Gompers, a pioneer of the U.S. labor movement, called the most basic needs of all: bread, work, and peace.

The inner logic of Isaac Newton's scientific revolution is now in serious question. Its awesome power may never be the same. If science is the religion of modern governance, a new kind of Reformation is at hand.

It's about time.

The earlier Reformation coincided with the invention of printing. That enabled Martin Luther's local action—fastening ninety-five theses "for the purpose of eliciting truth" to the door of

Frederick's Castle Church in Wittenberg on October 31, 1517—to be copied and circulated far and wide, provoking debates and controversy from which the authority of the medieval church never recovered.

The new Reformation is also powered by information technology: computers hitched to electronic telecommunications.

In Martin Luther's time, the sale of indulgences and other forms of corruption had already polluted the social fabric and weakened the authority of the medieval church over social affairs. In our time, the social fallout of science—the dangers of nuclear explosive power, the moral dilemmas inherent in biotechnology, the potential for irreversible climate change, the ambiguous miracles of informatics—has been advertised worldwide, inducing global second thoughts.

A Memorable Innovation

My second story is more personal, and begins less than forty years ago, in 1963. I was then an Assistant Secretary of State in President John F. Kennedy's State Department, responsible for relations with most of the fifty-three intergovernmental organizations to which the United States then belonged. One of these was WMO, the World Meteorological Organization. Dr. Robert M. White, then head of the U.S. Weather Service, was naturally our chief representative to that little-noticed agency. In the summer of 1963, to prepare for an upcoming WMO meeting, I invited Bob White and Herb Holloman, the Assistant Secretary of Commerce for Science and Technology, to lunch at the State Department.

With no idea what it might lead to, I started early in the meal to tease my expert colleagues: "You scientists and technologists, you never tell us institution-builders what manmade miracles are going to be possible, far enough ahead of time to allow us to wrap them in political and financial and administrative clothing, before they start running around naked!" As an experiment, I challenged them to tell me, before lunch was over and in words I could understand, what revolutions in weather forecasting were in store.

They did. By the time we parted, I was wide-eyed, and so were they. I had learned that in the decade of the 1960s, four new technologies would be deployed, which together could revolutionize weather forecasting. One was *picture-taking satellites*, keeping track of cloud systems from above, giving a synoptic view covering the whole world, supplemented by but not depending on observations from land, sea, aircraft, and balloons. Another was measurements from *remote-sensing satellites* of temperatures and air currents at places around the earth that couldn't be matched by observation from balloons or other probes launched from the earth's surface. A third was *communication satellites*, which would be able to get digitized data from anywhere to anywhere else in a big hurry. And the fourth breakthrough was about to be *much faster computers*, which could process the complex information coming in from all over the world and get it onto the forecasters' desks in time—that is, before the weather changed.

Over a second cup of coffee we looked together in awe at this prospect. The obvious policy conclusion occurred to us as a kind of simultaneous solution. If these new technologies could be pulled together into a workable world *system*, the human race would be able, for the first time in history, to think of the weather as a single envelope around the globe—the way God had presumably been thinking of it right along. But because the weather impertinently ignores the land frontiers and ocean jurisdictions we humans consider so important, such a system would require the cooperation of more than a hundred nations to make global forecasting work.

We decided, then and there, to launch a U.S. initiative at the next global assembly of the WMO, a few months away. I no longer remember who first suggested calling it the "World Weather Watch"—success always has multiple parents. A plan was developed by hardworking staffs in both departments. I was ready to authorize Bob White to launch it, and he was champing at the bit to sell it to national weather services around the world.

Then we got lucky. Another function of my bureau was to backstop the U.S. mission to the United Nations in New York, headed by an authentically great man: Adlai Stevenson, who had been governor of Illinois and twice (1952 and 1956) the Democratic candidate for president. Ambassador Stevenson, with help from me and support from Secretary of State Dean Rusk, was trying to persuade President Kennedy to go to New York that autumn to make an international policy speech to the U.N. General Assembly, in his capacity as chief of state of the host nation. The President was interested; the General Assembly was then a world forum without parallel, an impressive environment for a major policy speech. But he was petulant about the content of such an address. I don't want to go up there, he said in effect, and mouth all those clichés that are usually heard in U.N. speeches. Is there something fresh for me to say?

The opening was too inviting to pass up. "Well, Mr. President, we just happen to have developed a proposal for a World Weather Watch, using satellites our space program is launching. We were going to float it at the WMO, but why not float it at the General Assembly instead?"

After a few minutes' discussion, the President was more than receptive; he was so enthusiastic that I was puzzled at first. Afterwards the political barometers on the White House staff explained the tie-in with domestic politics. The President had received a heavy dose of editorial flak for announcing, in 1961, that the United States would put a man on the Moon before the end of the 1960s. We can't even clean up our urban slums, the editorial writers were writing, and this guy wants to go to the Moon! If President Kennedy could, at the U.N., hang up a new vision of a space-based system that would move us from chancy three-day weather forecasts to more dependable predictions five days ahead, he could dramatize the prospect that the exciting but expensive U.S. space program would benefit every farmer, every businessman, every picnicker, every citizen who needs to guess, with the help of the atmospheric sciences, what the weather is going to do next.

Thus it was that the World Weather Watch became one of the major Kennedy initiatives in the General Assembly in the autumn of 1963 (only a few weeks before the President was assassinated during a visit to Dallas). No one in the General Assembly, including the Soviet delegate, could think of any reason why it wasn't a splendid idea; it passed unanimously and was referred for action to the WMO. And there, Bob White and several other U.S. scientist-statesmen managed to arrange the endorsement and participation of nearly every country in the world. The two biggest data-collection centers, it was agreed, would be near Moscow and in Bethesda, Maryland, a suburb of Washington, D.C. And, because the politics of the World Weather Watch had been drained out through its approval by the U.N. General Assembly, no one at WMO felt the need to hold up the gathering global consensus by talking about Palestine, East Germany, Taiwan, or any of the other political issues then available to distract attention from action items being considered by the U.N.'s technical agencies.

By the late 1960s, the World Weather Watch was up and running—the satellites and ground stations communicating with each other, most of the world's nations contributing to the expenses and adding their local observations to the global data pool, the resulting information being converted into forecasts by thousands of meteorologists (and, on television, a good many pseudometeorologists) around the world. Even the People's Republic of China, which stayed aloof at first, in time sent a junior officer to deposit weather data at the Bethesda headquarters, sidling into the World Weather Watch without having to say they were mistaken to stay out when it was launched.

The lesson from this success story is clear. The way to avoid damaging fallout from science and technology is to invent the political, financial, and administrative framework for managing breakthroughs while the hardware (in this case, the picture-taking and remote-sensing satellites, the communications satellites, the faster computers) is still being procured and deployed.

Afterthought may be too late. The Manhattan Project provides a relevant warning. The story of the World Weather Watch suggests that it's possible, if we work hard at it, to stay ahead of the game.

Biotech's Ambiguous Attraction

After these (I hope illuminating) digressions, let's return to the extraordinary potentials of biology for tweaking human evolution itself. If I had my life to do all over again, I would be mightily tempted to become a biologist, opting for specialization in biotechnology. That way, I could be in on the ground floor of something really new: an effort to change the world by changing humanity itself.

The word is new, but *biotechnology* is as old as hunting, fishing, and cultivating. Whenever, way back in antiquity, silkworms were first invited by humans to munch on mulberry leaves to produce what is still the world's finest fiber, that was biotechnology.

Modern civilization produces an enormous volume of organic waste, the by-product of agriculture, animal husbandry, industry, and a couple of billion households. I've spent enough time with biotechnologists to be persuaded that there isn't any such thing as waste, only different kinds of raw materials we haven't yet learned to use. Carelessly disposed of, waste is at best a nuisance and at worst a community hazard. Carefully reused, it can produce energy (biogas), building materials, feed, food, and fiber.

A dozen years ago, I had the privilege of spending a few days with a world-class mushroom expert, Dr. S. T. Chang of the Chinese University in Hong Kong. All mushrooms really need, according to Dr. Chang, is darkness and waste. They can be grown in sawdust, corncobs, bagasse (what's left over when you harvest cane sugar), or tea leaves (after they've been used by a tea house). Using waste cultures, these Chinese scientists had grown straw mushrooms from spore to developed mushrooms in ten days. That's thirty-six crops a year, which may be some kind of world record.

I'm attracted not only by the productivity of biotech, but by its meaning for politics. Biotech is not a centralizing technology—like, say, fusion energy, which would require huge central power stations. Biotech seems much more likely to develop in an uncentralized way, on scattered farms and experiment stations, in millions of rural villages as they convert waste into biogas, in countless forests as people learn to plant fast-growing trees while they harvest old ones.

Even better news is that the new biosociety may help narrow the gap between rich and poor in a world where resentments about fairness are a prime source of conflict.

Most of the world's rich supply of biomass and most of the life-giving radiation from the sun are in the so-called poorer parts of the world. What's missing in "poor countries" is typically *not* the usable biological resources, but the educated brains to convert them into wealth. This "gives promise," said a study group of the World Academy of Art and Science in 1988, "that a world society focusing sharply on the constructive use of the bioresource can be a fairer world."

But . . . like every new scientific discovery or technological innovation, the news about the social fallout of biotechnology is ambiguous.

It's obviously useful in all sorts of ways as a weapon against disease. Yet the same science-and-technology can be used to spread disease to weaken enemy troops or obliterate a population deemed an enemy.

I learned early in life that the war against disease can go awry. When I was a young relief administrator for the U.N. in Italy just after World War II, we decided to show how the malaria-carrying anopheles mosquito could be wiped off the earth. We organized a demonstration on the island of Sardinia, spraying DDT from the air and poisoning mosquito-breeding ditches with an insecticide called Paris green. The operation was successful—we thought we killed every mosquito in Sardinia in 1946—but the patient lived on.

When the eradication strategy was tried on a larger scale in less remote areas, the anopheles mosquitoes developed an immunity to our biochemical warfare. And, to compound the backlash, our DDT turned out to have boomerang effects on the human populations we were trying to protect.

The propensity of science-and-technology to bite the hands that feed it has now been widely advertised. No longer can scientists operate in obscurity behind their laboratory walls and their specialized vocabularies. As they push past the frontiers of past ignorance, they have to carry the rest of us with them—or risk our instinctive reaction: if we don't understand it, it's probably dangerous, so stop!

Genetic Uncertainties

We can see this uncertainty of ours magnified in the headlines just now. Lots of Europeans are worried that genetically modified food may not be good for them. Most Americans still think it's OK, for example, to spray corn with chemicals that poison pests but don't poison people—though some of us worry when we hear that spraying cornfields in the Midwest might lay a deadly trap for the beautiful Monarch butterflies that migrate each year from their breeding grounds in Mexico to their summer vacation resorts in Canada.

So now the issue of genetically modified foods is a major controversy in transatlantic trade—and some big food producers are already trying to make sure the crops and animals they produce can be honestly advertised as *not* genetically modified, so they won't be blackballed in Europe.

The trouble is, most of agriculture requires human beings to make judgments about the plants they sow—which will grow faster, be less attractive to pests, taste better, last longer in storage, and so forth. Those judgments are based on centuries of trial and error and generations of agricultural science, which have taught farmers which crops are the best genetic bets.

In animal husbandry, breeding and selecting animals—that is, making judgments about genetic characteristics that lead to steaks, chops, poultry, and fish that grow faster, are tenderer and tastier— has been going on ever since farming turned out to be a more effi- cient way to produce food than hunting could ever be.

Nowadays, as scientists learn more and more about genes, and are more and more skillful at manipulating them, we consumers are learning that we have to make decisions we never had to make before. Is there a line to be drawn between selecting the juiciest steak or the fastest racehorse by observation and guesswork, and breeding cows and horses to bring the consumer's guess closer to a sure thing? If so, we've long since breached *that* borderline.

So, how much further do we consumers push the producers to go? I don't have any idea whether the cloned sheep called Dolly grows finer wool—or would taste better if she were slaughtered for mutton—than the product of a normal herd; her quality depends on that of the nameless sheep whose genes were used to bring her to life. If cloning were to produce better lamb and finer wool, and since we raise sheep to shear them for clothing and slaughter them for food, is cloning any less "natural" than any of the hundreds of other miracles of agricultural science we've already blessed with our choices in the marketplace?

I learned recently that they're cloning dogs at Texas A&M. As longtime dog-owners, my wife Lois and I could appreciate that. She would doubtless nominate her favorite chow for replication. I would offer up, if he were still alive, a cross-breed named Red, the handsomest, most intelligent, most likable dog I ever knew. Cloning a cross-breed might involve some technical problems, I don't know; but they couldn't present much more difficulty than Red's parents, an Irish setter and a cocker spaniel, had in conceiving him to begin with.

The main purpose in cloning is of course to try hard to understand how it works—so that, soon or late, it can be used to modify human evolution at human command. This also we have also been doing more and more in modern times—by swallowing medications and injecting drugs into our veins, by surgical intervention in our bodies and psychological intervention in our minds, by making deliberate changes in our local environments and causing inadvertent changes in the global atmosphere.

Just around the next corner, now that the human genome is being deciphered and catalogued, a whole new set of ethical puzzles awaits us in a moral quagmire.

Dicey Dilemmas

Some of the future uses of human genetics have come to be known as *reprogenetics*. That's defined, by Lee Silver at Princeton, as the use of genetic information or technology in an attempt by individuals to ensure or prevent the inheritance of particular genes in their child.

It's already technically possible for parents to choose which of their own genes to give to, or withhold from, their own children. The technique, known as preimplantation genetic diagnosis or PGD, is pretty expensive; so far, it's a perk for the affluent.

This is already being done to screen out fatal diseases—for example, if both parents are carriers of cystic fibrosis. It is hardly routine, but is made possible by in vitro fertilization (IVF): that is, combining the parents' sperm and eggs in a dish, testing each resulting embryo to find out which *don't* contain the disease gene, then implanting in the mother's womb only the embryos with the safe genes.

Soon, according to Professor Silver, parents may be able to modify the genes in their embryos so that their children can be born with genes they *couldn't* get naturally. But these are still what can be called "natural" genes because *other* children get them naturally. Embryo selection doesn't modify the human genome, and Lee Silver is relaxed about it. "It just allows parents to select one microscopic embryo over another," he says. "It's equivalent to placing the genetic dice on the table rather than throwing them for a random outcome."

The further ahead you try to look, the dicier are the dilemmas we could face.

Embryo selection already gives rise to a host of ethical questions—more than enough to create full employment for those who hang out shingles as bioethicists. They range from the almost trivial—is it "fair" for parents to select for a taller basketball player (assuming they can persuade their grown-up embryo to play basketball) than their neighbors can afford?—to fundamental questions about fairness in society at large.

If only the affluent can place their dice on the table, while others still take their chances with random genetic selection, won't that increase the already alarming gap between rich and poor? To offset the new unfairnesses, some political leaders will doubtless want to bring the government in, to level the genetic playing field. The cost could dwarf the most ambitious universal health plan ever devised; the enforcement risks intruding politics into love affairs.

Let's carry this speculation only one policy step further. Once it becomes possible to provide nonhuman genes to the embryo of a child, the prospect looms of a master race with growing wealth and a declining concern for the rest of humankind. Professor Silver, indeed, foresees a world of "severed humanity," in which all common heritage between the genetically enhanced and the genetically deprived is gone.

This is still more science fiction than science, just now. But it's worth listening to the writers of science fiction; some of them have an uncanny aptitude for guessing right about what might happen if we don't watch out.

Wouldn't it be better for all of us—those of you who are prospective parents and those who, like me, no longer produce children but can still produce policies and principles—to think hard about reprogenetics while most of its consequences are still more fancy than fact?

Catching Up and Speeding Up

The antidote to the social fallout of science is just that: hard thinking about the futures we want before the inner logic of science saddles us with a future we won't want. This doesn't mean putting science in a straitjacket. It means doing our social thinking *in parallel* with the thinking of scientists—so we don't have to keep playing catch-up. Unlike the Manhattan Project. More like the World Weather Watch.

Breakthroughs in social thinking, moreover, will have to come faster and faster, since the natural sciences keep accelerating the pace of change. As I was editing this essay for publication, the two teams that are trying to map the human genome announced an important discovery: that we humans have about one-third as many genes as scientists had previously thought.

The clear implication is that what each human gene can do is more complicated than had been assumed. And this suggests that the relationships among the more functionally complex genes, and the proteins and other substances they produce in our bodies, may be a lot more complicated than even the experts on such complications have thought hard about.

The tools we have to help us think about science are also improving with exponential speed. Dr. J. Craig Venter, the scientist who heads the Celera Genomics team, says that the time and energy he once spent over ten years studying one gene can now be collapsed (with much faster computers and also a much better understanding of the context) into fifteen minutes. Can we social thinkers demonstrate a comparable increase in productivity?

As the British economist Barbara Ward once wrote about a similarly puzzling enigma, human impacts on the global environment: "We do not know. We have the duty to hope."

Commentary on Chapter Eight

During his long and active life as a "practical visionary," Willis Harman mutated from an education as an electrical engineer to become one of the early "students of the future," a thoughtful writer in global perspective, and first president of the Institute of Noetic Sciences in California.

When he died in 1997, I wrote this essay to capture in my own idiom two of the ideas he and I had discussed at length early in the 1990s: about intuition as an essential stepping stone to wisdom, and about chaos theory and its relevance for analysis of social and political complexity.

In Willis Harman's way of thinking, two ideas seemed to be central. I found them so congenial I came to regard them as my ideas too.

One idea was that everything is related to everything else—a universal connectedness that combines material observation with spiritual experience, and quite deliberately blurs the distinction between the two. Modern Western science has focused on what can be learned from systematic observation and experimentation, with an intellectual rigor that withholds the accolade of "truth" from what cannot be proven by the scientific method. Yet there seem to be many human experiences, and not only in dreams, that cannot aspire to the credentials of scientific proof yet are nevertheless vivid, relevant, and useful in day-to-day living and planning ahead, for individuals, groups, and communities—and that are therefore, in some larger sense, also true.

The other idea was a hunch about the nature of the transition we all are in—"a shift," he called it, "in the locus of authority from external to internal." He sensed a "growing disenchantment with external authorities and increasing reliance on intuitive, inner wisdom and authority." He resonated with what he perceived as a more and more widespread realization that "we create our own reality," that we are "co-creators" of the world we live in, and that "ultimate cause is to be sought not in the physical, but in consciousness."

He was not challenging the scientific method as such; it had been, in fact, an important part of his own professional preparation. What he seemed to be saying in his most recent writings was that scientific rationality simply didn't, couldn't, go far enough to explain the way human beings are able to think, and in consequence to act. This led him to raise interesting—to some, disturbing—questions, not so much about means as about meaning. And it led me to think even harder about intuition and chaos as meaningful if mysterious aspects of a leader's mindset.

8

Intuition and Chaos in the Real World

The Role of Intuition

Most of what we learn in organized systems—in families, in schools and colleges, in professional training, even in education for leadership roles—has to do with the uniquely human capacity to reason. But much of what we actually accomplish results from the application of wisdom, which is a mysterious fusion of rational thinking with nonrational thinking. So it's worth more than a few moments to think hard about how we think to achieve the wisdom to act.

How does your mind work?

After three hundred years of scientific rationalism, experts can answer half of that question, the easy half. We know how to train minds to argue from cause to effect. We can compare costs with benefits. We can guess at a hypothesis and create experiments, or gather statistics, to prove or disprove it.

We can bring people together in organizations to add value and create wealth—though we are not yet very good at distributing the wealth fairly. We are even beginning to figure out how to change ourselves, by nutrition and exercise, by drugs and vitamins, by psychiatric and genetic intervention.

It's the other half of the mind, the subconscious mind in action, that still puzzles us. That other half must be important: it's what we mostly use to imagine futures, create goals, and make decisions in government and business and academies and associations and clubs and families and our personal lives.

Like physicians who can name what they don't know how to treat, we give names to this mysterious yet dominant half of our psyche. We speak of our subconscious, of gut feelings, educated guesswork, ethical hunch, imagination, inspiration, grace, guidance from above, the answer to prayer, the Holy Spirit. For now, let's call it *intuition*.

When I start to write something, I don't usually know just what I am going to say or how. I may have an inchoate theme in mind— a happening worth relating, a fragment of fresh knowledge, a reaction to what's just happened in my community or in world affairs or in my personal relations. I brood for several hours, dipping into my own notes and other people's writings collected (often over many years) to cover the contingency that I might want to think hard, some day, about the chosen topic.

Then suddenly, quite literally in a flash, I know what I want to say and how to get it written. I've turned on (don't ask me how) the other half of my mind. I've exercised my intuition—and it has imposed on my plodding conscious reasoned thinking a super-logic, a way of ordering reality that is clearly much more than the sum of its rational parts.

Consider your own case. You have been puzzling fruitlessly about some wrenching dilemma, some seemingly insoluble problem, some sour personal relationship. You give up for the moment, and decide to sleep on it. The next morning, while brushing your teeth or waiting for the coffee to brew, your conscious mind returns to the puzzle with a fresh insight, the germ of a new idea, a suddenly obvious next step to be taken.

While you were sleeping, your always active brain was busy. But freed from the constraints of those rational ways of thought drilled into your conscious mind by years in school and on the job, the deep-down part of your mind made some nonrational connections and a leap of imagination, and served up to your wakening consciousness a fresh line of thought.

Intuition is "knowing without knowing how you know," as Lonnie Helgeson puts it. Everyone does this all the time. We resist talking about it out loud because it doesn't seem practical in a world so dominated by scientific rationalism we even pretend that politics and human relations are sciences, sort of. But now, intuition is coming into vogue as we discover the practical uses of visioning and imaging—constructing in our mind's eye future scenarios that suggest changes in human behavior starting right now.

We are discovering, too, that the conscious release of the unconscious mind, the key that unlocks the jail of reason, is not reserved for an elite of saints, priests, master teachers, and charismatic leaders. Vision and revelation and guidance are paths to empowerment available to anyone and everyone who is open to them.

Intuition is not, of course, a substitute for reason. Of all its synonyms, I like *educated hunch* the best. It implies what I believe is basic: that the wider and deeper the base of reasoned knowledge, the wiser and more useful will be the intuitions that sparkle beyond its reach.

The burgeoning interest in intuitive leadership may stem from a dawning realization that all of us, and especially those who presume to take the lead, need to cope with what cannot be tackled rationally because it hasn't happened yet.

Shirley Hufstedler, who was the first U.S. Secretary of Education, explained it this way: In other times most people were trained to apply known methods to familiar tasks, first in agriculture then in industry. But in the changing knowledge environment, we need to educate our young people—and ourselves—for future tasks, for what's never been done before, for what cannot be explained but has to be imagined. In that kind of learning, the ratio of intuition to reasoning is bound to keep rising.

That ratio is even higher for people who take the lead in communities large and small: They have to envision a future in order to point the way.

Intuition in Action

In the business world, serious discussion of intuitive leadership used to be regarded as far-out, too remote from rational calculations and profit margins. But in the late 1980s, some U.S. corporate leaders started to spend good bottom-line money to help their rising executives learn to make maximum use of their intuitive brainpower. As it began to appear that companies interesting themselves in intuitive leadership were also doing well in the marketplace, the idea traveled fast.

Some human resources executives greeted this new approach to mindpower with caution, rather like cats circling a new kind of food. And no wonder. "The word 'intuition' not only refers to an ability worth having," Willis Harman wrote some years ago. "It also signals the hearer that the individual using it is open to rethinking the entire business enterprise."

In government and public affairs, where plans are even more intuitive and outcomes less quantifiably rational, the minds of those who presume to lead must be even more open to nonrational insights and leaps of imagination.

In a U.S. Supreme Court opinion in 1905, Oliver Wendell Holmes wrote wisely about intuitive leadership: "General propositions do not decide concrete cases. The decision will depend on a judgment or intuition more subtle than any articulate major premise."

Since most of my experience has been in the practice and observation of international affairs, perhaps it's best that I retrieve from my random access memory some examples of what led to my interest in intuitive leadership.

When I worked in the U.S. State Department, I noticed that whenever a foreign-policy question could be addressed by rational argument and reasoned compromise, the matter was settled by brokerage at the subcabinet level or below. The issues that went to the Secretary of State or the President were those that could be decided any of several ways, each way eminently reasonable. So the top political leaders mostly seemed to be engaged full-time in using their intuition.

A backward glance suggests that major moves on the international chessboard are based less on rational analysis before the fact than on a political leader's intuition, or ethical hunch, ahead of time.

I once had occasion to ask Jean Monnet, author of the "Schuman Plan" for a European Coal-Steel Authority as a first step toward an integrated European Community, who had helped him think up that imaginative and successful initiative. His rehearsal of that bit of history included one memorable piece of practical philosophy. "I certainly didn't consult any experts on coal and steel," he told me. "They would have said it was impossible."

Most of the time, of course, policymakers have to be awake, the rational half of their minds at full alert. But the need to free the imaginative subconscious from the constraints of the conscious mind is so great—especially on matters of high policy—that a case can be made for daydreaming in committees.

On one legendary occasion John J. McCloy, a top official in the War Department, dozed off during a meeting where President Franklin Roosevelt was trying to decide (while the United States was still neutral in World War II) how best to help the European allies, and how to present this "foreign aid" to a still skeptical U.S. public. The President, an incorrigible tease, abruptly awakened his sleeping subordinate with a question: "Well, Jack, what do you think we ought to do?"

McCloy opened one eye. "Mr. President, I think we should be the arsenal of democracy." Roosevelt's acceptance of this advice was just as rapid, and just as intuitive. "From now on, Jack, that phrase is mine, not yours."

In early 1943 Harry Hopkins, President Roosevelt's closest confidant, was helping FDR prepare his State of the Union message. Targets for war production were to be set in that speech, and Hopkins cited a report from a panel of experts that the United States economy, by straining every nerve, could produce twenty-five thousand military aircraft the following year. Twenty-five thousand doesn't sound like enough, Roosevelt said to Hopkins; let's double it and add ten. The aircraft industry didn't quite meet the new target of sixty thousand planes that year. But spurred by a leader's act of intuitive leadership, it did turn out forty-nine thousand planes, almost double what the experts had said was the limit of possibility.

When in June 1950 the North Koreans rumbled south across the 38th parallel in their Soviet-made tanks, the first American reaction was to get the U.N. Security Council (in the serendipitous absence of the Soviet delegation) to label the North Korean invasion an "armed attack." President Truman returned from a weekend in Missouri to meet with his top advisers at dinner in Blair House, across the street from a White House under repair. Just before dinner started, Truman was heard to declare, softly, "We can't let the U.N. down."

The President called first on Secretary of Defense Louis Johnson and military chief of staff General Omar Bradley. They advised against reacting militarily to the North Korean move. Dean Acheson, the Secretary of State, then produced a strong and cogent brief, urging that the United States take the lead in carrying into action a U.N. riposte to this clear violation of a dividing line established by international agreement. Truman, who probably consulted his advisers in that order because his intuition had already told him that strong action was imperative, backed Acheson, and the Korean War was on—with a U.N. Security Council mandate to a U.N. force led by a U.S. commander.

Later, when after much uncertainty the tide had turned in favor of the U.N. forces, their U.S. commander General Douglas MacArthur was frustrated by the insistence of his commander-in-chief, the President, that he refrain from chasing the North Korean troops all the way up to the Chinese border on the Yalu River, for fear that would bring the Chinese even more heavily into the fray. Without notice to the Joint Chiefs of Staff or the Truman administration, MacArthur wrote a letter of protest to the Republican speaker of the House of Representatives.

The President's press secretary, Roger Tubby, first saw this news on the AP ticker. He tore it off and hurried to the Oval Office, where Truman happened to be sitting alone. Without a word, Tubby placed the news item on the President's desk. Truman read it quickly and (Tubby told me later) compressed into one pithy sentence his intuitive reaction based on a precise constitutional analysis. "The son-of-a-bitch can do that to Harry Truman," said Harry Truman, "but he can't do that to the President of the United States!" The rapid end to General MacArthur's military career was foreordained.

Most of the inspired initiatives in our international relations have been similarly based, at first, more on a political leader's ethical hunch than on rational staff work before the fact. Henry David Thoreau said it more elegantly: "We must walk consciously only part way toward our goal, and then leap in the dark to our success."

President John F. Kennedy's 1961 decision to set a 1969 deadline for placing a man on the Moon; President Dwight Eisenhower's calls for "open skies" and "atoms for peace"; Secretary of State George Marshall's 1947 commencement speech at Harvard about European recovery (now remembered as the Marshall Plan, though it wasn't "planned" ahead of time); and President Truman's "Point Four" proposal to extend technical aid to the world's less developed nations—all these were leaps into the unknown, policy judgments unwarranted by the then-available expert advice. In each case the major planning effort came *after* the policy decision.

Because my job in Washington at the time was to manage U.S. foreign aid to East Asian countries, I attended the first interdepartmental meeting held to carry into action "Point Four" of the President's 1949 inaugural address earlier that week. Around a long table in the State Department sat all the government's ranking experts on technical assistance to less developed countries. None of us had been consulted, or even knew in advance, about President Truman's intention to include "Point Four" in his speech. Assistant Secretary of State Willard Thorp, who had also had no advance notice, slowly looked around our bewildered gathering. "Well, gentlemen," he said with a smile, "what do you suppose the President meant?" *Then* the planning began.

Intuitive leadership is of course no guarantee of success. The 1961 attempt to invade Cuba by indirection (at the Bay of Pigs) was a fiasco because President Kennedy took on faith a plan inherited from his predecessor President Eisenhower—and neglected to ask the Joint Chiefs of Staff for a sober assessment of whether the proposed military deployment of Cuban exiles, planned by a CIA unit headed by an economist, would work. President Lyndon B. Johnson was so intuitively clear about the downside of being the first U.S. president to lose a war that he effectively waved off advice to "declare victory and get out" of Vietnam, as suggested by Senator Aiken of Vermont and others—until he suddenly widened the circle of advisers early in 1968, and in consequence announced on March 31, 1968, that he would not be running for reelection that fall. President Richard Nixon shared a similar reluctant intuition for most of his first term in office, before he finally permitted the war to be lost by negotiation. President Jimmy Carter authorized a hostage snatch in Iran, but didn't make rationally sure the helicopter task force was equal to the task. President Ronald Reagan (and people speaking for him) mired the U.S. government in the Iran-contra mess, where emotional attachment to a cause kept elbowing rational analysis offstage.

My purpose in evoking all these memories is to illustrate that political leadership is by its nature intuitive. Intuition is obviously not always better than reasoning; rationality doesn't always work so well either. Each needs to be available as a prism through which the decision maker can look hard at the other.

It is the political leader's mandate both to view with a skeptical intuitive eye the advisers' rational analysis and to supply the forward-looking vision that distinguishes the person who has to act from the advisory prophets of doom.

Chaos to the Rescue?

It was in the first year of my so-called retirement, fourteen years ago at age seventy, that I suddenly got interested in the contribution of chaos theory to the study and practice of leadership. The life of the mind—my mind, at least—seems to grow by nonlinear accidents, coincidence, serendipity. Three happenings early in 1988 opened, for me, ways of thinking about the previously unthinkable.

First came a briefing at the National Center for Atmospheric Research (I was then on its Board of Trustees) by mathematicians who showed gorgeous moving images of fractal landscapes and explained the new, nonlinear science called *chaos* in ways that, astonishingly, could be taken in by a mind that had had trouble with eighth-grade arithmetic.

Shortly after that I had a chance, in Paris at a meeting of the Club of Rome (of which I'm a member), to meet and listen to Ilya Prigogine, the ranking philosopher of "instability"—his patented version of chaos. The next day, on the long flight home, I passed up the airline movie and read James Gleick's new book *Chaos*, a dense but lucid story about the new science.

The word *chaos* had long been in my vocabulary. It defined what an educated person, educated in linear thinking by the logic (and the prestige) of the scientific method, couldn't quite understand. *Chaos* described that inferno of unfathomable complexity lying just beyond the flat world of empirical evidence.

But chaos turned out to have its own patterns and probabilities. What had always seemed random—outbreaks of measles in New York City, the fluctuations of Canada's lynx population, the ups and downs of cotton prices—shows a complicated rhythm if your statistical database stretches back far enough.

The same is true, apparently, of physical things and abstract numbers. They look random only when you stand too close to them, look at them piece by piece, in the reductionist tradition of sciences that chop knowledge up into so-called manageable chunks and thus make the knowledge unmanageable.

Gleick explained: "The microscopic pieces were perfectly clear; the macroscopic behavior remained a mystery. The tradition of looking at systems locally—isolating the mechanisms and then adding them together—was beginning to break down. For pendulums, for fluids, for electronic circuits, for lasers, knowledge of the fundamental equations no longer seemed to be the right kind of knowledge at all."

The author leavened his weighty loaf by describing some of the real-life mathematical explorers who had been learning how to combine speedy computers with scientific irreverence, posing and asking questions never asked before. (How long is a coastline? Depends on the length of your measuring rod, which determines the number of measurements you have to take.)

It was an effective literary device, those corduroy jackets and unkempt laboratories, those young scientists walking in the wilds (on company time) in search of inspiration, those intellectual frontiersmen with their very human jealousies about who got there first.

I wondered, though, as I tried to understand this fresh way of thinking: Gleick's "great man" theory of scientific advance (women were scarce in his narrative) must have left a good many other scientists, and their graduate students, wondering why they didn't also find their names immortalized in the index of the "new science." Is the progress of nonlinear studies really so linear, leading with such logical positivism from one genius to another?

Just the same, Gleick's story was full of insightful characters, who had in common their delight in tweaking the nose of the scientific establishment. I had often noticed, in half a century of study and practice, that my favorite leaders seemed to share a sense of humor, a talent for irony, and a delight in turning conventional wisdom on its head.

The presiding geniuses of this new science certainly specialized in irreverence. Mitchell Feigenbaum, as a young post-doc, explaining to his professors why he didn't finish a paper on a manageable problem: "Oh, I understood it." Enrico Fermi exclaiming, "It does not say in the Bible that all laws of nature are expressible linearly!" And Murray Gell-Mann, poking fun at academic politics: "Faculty members are familiar with a certain kind of person who looks to the mathematicians like a good physicist and looks to the physicists like a good mathematician. Very properly, they do not want that kind of person around."

A Hunch About Chaos Theory

For me, the revelations about this new science served as a kind of scientific experiment. Before I even started trying to understand it, I had a hunch. (A scientist would have called it a hypothesis.) I've now concluded that the chaos experts were validating my intuition. The only trouble was that most of them described it in such impenetrable language.

My hunch was this: the chaos enthusiasts were discovering that their world of numbers and physical things is not, after all, so different from the untidy world of human relations.

We who study society have known all along, haven't we, that systems are never regular, never (despite what we fondly call scientific polling) reliably predictable? Yet the chaotic confusions of politics and administration do yield to analysis, do prove to be what one chaos analyst calls "randomness with its own underlying order."

Just like swirling clouds or oscillating pendulums, human history never does quite repeat itself. Yet the study of patterns derived from the messy relations of people with each other down through the ages does somehow help us decide what to do starting tomorrow morning.

Indeed, what I found most interesting about the "chaos chic" of the 1980s was to realize the new discoveries were so counterintuitive that they were not even suspected, or were dismissed as noise, for most of the history of science.

In any event, the mathematicians and natural scientists seemed to be discovering, and demonstrating with complex equations, what practitioners of politics, planning, business management, and public administration had long known by instinct and experience, trial and error—or even by reading Lao-tzu. For example:

It matters where you start. Chaos language is admittedly fancier ("sensitive dependence on initial conditions"), but care in selecting your starting point is hardly a blinding revelation about economic and social process.

The compartmentalization of the vertical disciplines gets in the way of understanding reality. Central to the executive function in every organization is the uphill struggle to think and act integratively in the face of expert fragmentation.

We had better not neglect the "externalities"—those naggingly relevant factors that don't fit into our logical modes of thinking, those "bits of messiness that interfere with a neat picture," so you put them on a shelf to think about some other time. Those bits of messiness are often near the center of the leadership function in a complex society, because the center is where the human beings are.

A final example: *The biggest danger to systematic thinking is information entropy.* We sort of knew that already, didn't we? As the mail comes inexorably in and the unanswered phone calls pile up, we are obsessed, overwhelmed with facts and ideas that multiply disorder. Our newly quickened capacity to process information sometimes seems to make things worse.

Yet as we learn to use the instruments of the knowledge revolution, we find they can also help us select the nuggets from the slagheap and thus reduce our information entropy. When I'm feeling especially confused about a new problem, I usually find that what's needed is not more facts or even new ideas but a more focused effort to integrate the facts and ideas that are already lying around—that look chaotic only because I haven't yet succeeded in bringing them all together in my mind. As usual, Lao-tzu said it more succinctly: "When the whole is lost, the parts need names."

"The disorderly behavior of simple systems [acts] as a creative process," James Gleick wrote in his provocative book a dozen years ago. That is, I believe, why those of us whose lifework is bringing people together to make something different happen find that the creative disorder is part of what's fun about it.

There is a message here from the social nonsciences to the newly exhilarated scientists of chaos: Welcome to the club!

In Love With Complexity

Why am I telling you all this? Because there is a lesson here for those of us whose chosen super-profession is (or will in future be) to point the way and take the lead. The lesson is that if you're serious about being a leader, you should arrange to fall in love, early and often, with chaos and complexity.

You have to come to think of complications as the charming norm, not as passing aberrations from a tidy pattern. As you strive to make some restless complexity more understandable and you're tempted to simplify it, remember what Albert Einstein said about equations: that they should be "as simple as possible, but not one bit simpler."

If a situation seems too chaotic for you to understand, that doesn't mean it's more chaotic than the reality with which you're going to have to deal. It may just be a clue for you to widen your lens and deepen your thoughts.

As complexity grows (and it will), more and more of your friends and colleagues—not to mention competitors and others—are going to drop out of the race to keep up with it. To whom will they then look for clarification, and for guidance about what to do? If you are still in the race, thinking hard even if you don't yet have the answers, that's what qualifies you for the leader's role. If you too drop out, the would-be followers will quickly look elsewhere for the leadership they need.

No matter how chaotic the puzzle that confronts you seems to be, your task is to get your good mind around all of it—including especially those "bits of messiness" that don't (at first) seem to fit in anywhere.

Please note that I said *your* mind, not your assistant's mind or the collective mind of a planning staff. I have mentioned President Kennedy's most important strategic error, the fiasco called the Bay of Pigs. He had as steep a learning curve as anyone I've known, and he obviously learned an important lesson about leadership: If the leader is not personally engaged in the staff work that leads to an important decision, he is merely presiding while others decide.

Eighteen months later, when he faced up to the Soviet missiles in Cuba, he immersed himself in the staff work, personally weighing the alternative courses of action, insisting that the probable consequences of each be thought all the way through. Even so, the "quarantine" scenario he selected, a complex mix of diplomatic moves and military maneuvers, was dicey. Yet in the end, it worked. The Soviet leader Nikita Khrushchev turned his ships around to avoid challenging the hemispheric blockade of Cuba, and after a long negotiation removed the nuclear warheads from an island ninety miles from the U.S. coastline.

Only by Thinking and Imagining . . .

"Presiding while others decide." Plenty of prominent people do just that, and are even well paid for it. Some have titles like chairman or president or even lord chancellor or emperor. But it isn't their titles that make them leaders. It's the excellence of what they personally do—especially in thinking through what to do and why, and inducing others to do their part—that qualifies them for what Woodrow Wilson called the "exalted" title of leader.

Above all, the real-world complexity your brain must try to match bids you put no restraints on your good mind or your soaring imagination. Your brain is the only instrument you can trust that can think straight even when all the lines you're watching are curves, the only tool that makes it possible for you, unlike most people, to examine what looks like randomness and intuit its underlying order. And it's only by using your imagination that you can escape the thinking person's most dangerous mindset: to consider only those futures that can be readily extrapolated from where we are today.

Your personality, your winning smile, your sexiness, or your attractive voice may seem persuasive leadership assets. But it's by thinking and imagining that you can decide where you want to go, and persuade others to come along in a nobody-in-charge environment.

Part II

On Being a Leader

Commentary on Chapter Nine

My education in the commonsense study of the future was greatly enhanced by my close association with John and Magda McHale in the 1970s and 1980, and after John's death with Magda as a close associate in the World Academy of Art and Science.

This remarkable couple pioneered in thinking of the future not just as what was likely to happen but as what we could make happen. John McHale's deep yet readable book, *The Future of the Future* (New York: Braziller, 1969), is one of the books I can honestly say changed my life. The McHales did their share of forecasting, but their definition of futures studies was the systematic imagination of *alternative futures,* from which I, we, our community, our nation, could select the most desirable outcome—and work hard to bring it about, starting tomorrow morning.

Studying the future is no longer a far-out, fringe activity. It is widely and reputably practiced in corporations, government agencies, universities, citizens' leagues, serious think tanks, and thriving consultancies.

I have never described myself as a futurist, but I have sometimes been so characterized by others, simply because I have preferred to aim so many of my writings and actions at what hasn't happened yet. My 1972 book, *The Future Executive,* sold well from the bookstore of the World Future Society. Ever since then, I have considered the community of futurists as one of the many intersecting circles in which I live my professional life. So perhaps it was natural that I came to think of leaders as active futurists, and of budding futurists as potential leaders.

9

The Leader as Futurist

The Art of Conjecture

There are countless definitions of leadership, but all of them seem to agree on one thing all leaders do: they peer into the future, as a basis for pointing the way toward desirable futures. In modern times, peering into the future is no longer left to ancient prophets and Asian seers. The club of students of society contains a growing number of people who try, overtly and professionally, to think hard about what is yet to come.

There is of course some danger here. Precisely because the focus is what hasn't happened yet, the topic under study is bound to be a subjective product of the human imagination. Many people attracted to "futures studies" are lured into making predictions—and it does seem to be easier, more fun, and more profitable to imagine bad news than good news. The greatest temptation of all is to predict catastrophe. It makes headlines, sells books, funds lecture tours and travel to distant conferences. If she were living today, Cassandra could not be ignored by order of Apollo; she would be a syndicated columnist and a sought-after consultant.

But leaders who presume to point the way are bound to be skeptical of guesses that suggest a future less desirable than the present. People are moved, as one of my graduate students creatively put it,

by "a cocktail of fear and hope." It is usually the leader's job to provide the hope.

The systematic study of the future is a very recent phenomenon
in the long history of thinking. "The intellectual construction of a
likely future is a work of art," one of the early pioneers, Bertrand de
Jouvenel, wrote in 1967. He called it, not planning or forecasting,
but "the art of conjecture."

Since then the snowballing speed and memory of computers,
combined with the growing reliability of speedy telecommunications, have made it possible to ask what-if questions about very
complex systems—the global climate, nuclear weapons effects, population growth, money values, labor productivity, markets for goods
and services, threats to the environment. Juggling models of the
future has become a familiar mode of thought widely practiced in
every community.

All around us, the metaphor of Year 2000—and latterly, more
safely distant goal lines: 2015, 2025—became a popular framework
for planning by schools, scholars, public authorities, legislatures,
corporations, policy analysts, one-issue lobbies, and citizen's groups.
Simulation techniques are routinely taught in graduate schools of
business, planning, and public affairs. Trouble in the global environment that can still be foreseen only in the calculations of
nuclear physicists or atmospheric chemists has come to be cover-
story fare. Millions now use popularized models of the future as
guidance on whether or when to have babies, practice safe sex, buy
aerosol hair spray, eat more fiber, or even plan an outdoor picnic for
the day after tomorrow.

Peering into the future is thus accepted, unassailable in its purpose if not in some of its methods of analysis. *Futurist* is now a
mostly respected self-designation. It is even used, here and there, as
a corporate job description. Earl Joseph, a Minnesotan who thinks
about technological futures for a living, had the title of "staff futurist" when he worked for the old Sperry Corporation. And all of this
has happened in less than half a century.

To call oneself a futurist requires no special license or common credentials, so the tag did at first attract some strange bedfellows. At a 1980 meeting in Toronto, billed modestly as the First Global Conference on the Future, I was accosted during a coffee break by a disheveled young man who wanted to know whether I loved Jesus (which I did) and was ready (which I wasn't) for the end of the world the following Tuesday. But in wrapping up that same meeting, Maurice Strong—the cheerful Canadian businessman and international public executive—got things back into perspective with his closing comment: "The bad news is that the world is coming to an end. The good news is—not yet, and not necessarily."

Sirens to Resist

Those who would peer into the future have to learn to turn aside from some tempting siren songs.

One siren bids the futurist to commit the original analytical sin, which is to mistake current megatrends for future destiny. In the early 1970s, it was widely believed that we were about to run out of food, soil, energy, and fresh water. We haven't yet—partly, to be sure, because the havoc criers cried havoc.

Another siren tells us that what cannot be counted is an *externality*—that is, a disturbingly relevant factor that doesn't fit into one's current way of thinking, and so is shelved to think about some other time. But of course the real world is not neatly quantitative. What cannot be counted will often count more than what can.

Yet another siren teaches that all resources are natural. Some dedicated number-crunchers have had trouble thinking of information, imagination, invention, and innovation as resources, perhaps because they are so hard to measure. But in the advanced postindustrial economies, and increasingly in all economies, information is now clearly the primary raw material for economic and social development, and for defense systems too.

An early illusion, now discredited, was that "the future" was a new subject, a new field of knowledge to be organized in a new kind of academic department.

In the flush of the early space explorations, there arose a similar delusion, that outer space was a new subject, to be distinguished (and thus separated) from others by developing its own language and its own academic high priests. It didn't take long for the space enthusiasts to realize that space was not a new subject but a new *place*, a fascinating and hostile environment presenting new challenges to all the familiar fields and disciplines—physics and chemistry and mathematics and materials science and engineering and medicine and nutrition and physiology and psychology and economics and law . . . and politics.

The study of the future, at its best, has likewise developed as a fresh angle of vision on the whole range of human knowledge—and a new reason to thread together the compartments into which we have divided the life of the mind.

The way to turn aside these temptations is not to try to predict a unique and inevitable future, but to practice instead what is now called *imaging*—fashioning constructive alternative futures, then working back to preferred outcomes to guide decisions about what we ought to be doing, starting today, to bring them to pass. That is why it makes sense to treat what hasn't happened yet as a plural noun, as in "futures studies," the World Futures Studies Federation, and the British journal *Futures*.

But the prime temptation is always lurking in the wings. Among the conceivable futures for a person, group, nation, or civilization, it is still the catastrophic threat—the nuclear holocaust, the poisoned Earth, the atmospheric heat trap—that wins the ratings contest.

The trouble with accentuating the negative is that each new theory, each fresh scientific discovery, each technological innovation, penetrates the popular mind as a problem to be avoided, with no corresponding opportunity to be grasped. That mindset can paralyze the collective will to tackle the new kinds of problems that pose the greatest threats to the human species. These are the problems (global warming and AIDS are examples both current and choice) that are not only global in their reach but also behavioral in their solution—that is, they will require literally millions of people to stop doing something, or do something different, or both.

Perils of Extrapolation

Intellectual curiosity is a hallmark of executive leadership. One reason is that it enhances the leader's capacity to take with a grain of salt the descriptions of a glum future that litter the desk, shout from the local media, and punctuate conversations with colleagues.

The central executive in any enterprise is surrounded with gloomily reluctant experts saying the best thing to do is to study the problem some more. The academic executive, I found, has even readier access than others to a wider range of more systematic extrapolators of the disastrous consequences bound to flow from whatever action is proposed.

The reluctant colleagues may even include scholars who are making good royalties by converting current trends into future destiny. The most breathless of these computerized Cassandras seem very often to be wrong, and I have puzzled a good deal about the abnormal frequency of predictive error. The problem may just be that, as Isaiah Berlin wrote long ago, "The experts cannot know enough."

Keeping up with trends in one's own field is difficult enough, and experts are almost bound to assume that the factors they don't have time to study will cancel out the factors they have studied but don't understand. That leaves only one golden line of extrapolation from the corner of the complexity the specialist really does know something about—and each specialized projection, carried far enough into the future, leads to the Apocalypse.

The U.S. statisticians who underestimated the effects of development in depressing population growth are only the most obvious examples of that common statistical error, which is to assume that what you know will not be stood on its head by what you don't know.

The future-oriented leader, on the other hand, knows by instinct what the souls in Dante's *Inferno* learned to their sorrow: they could see clearly what lay far in the future, but things blurred as they drew nearer. A leader learns to mistrust expert predictions, especially when they are so long-range that when the eventual disaster is due, the forecaster—and, if the prediction is correct, all the readers too—may be dead. Or, if not dead, the forecaster might at least hope to be retired, looking fondly back on a long record of accuracy like that ancient retiree from the Research Department of the British Foreign Office who served from 1903 to 1950 and boasted thus at his retirement ceremony: "Year after year the worriers and fretters would come to me with awful predictions of the outbreak of war. I denied it each time. And I was only wrong twice."

Mark Twain was hard on the extrapolators of his era. "In the space of one hundred and seventy-six years the lower Mississippi has shortened itself 242 miles," he wrote. "That is an average of one mile and a third per year. [So] any person can see that 742 years from now the lower Mississippi will be only a mile and three-quarters long."

"There is something fascinating about science," he added. "One gets such wholesale returns of conjecture out of such a trifling investment of fact."

The bad news about the sins of extrapolation is that in most fields—in economics or military tactics or scientific discovery or industrial technology—the past is simply not a reliable guide to the future. Change is too kaleidoscopic, too various, too complicated, too simultaneous—in a word, too human—to be arranged in linear logic from cause to effect. But—here's the good news—those who preach and practice the arts of politics and administration don't have the same problem at all. They can have a pretty good idea what is going to happen next, because in this business of human cooperation the verities are something like eternal.

In America's most famous op-ed newspaper articles, *The Federalist Papers,* some of what Alexander Hamilton wrote about economic policy now seems quaint, archaic, the speculations of leaders of an underdeveloped country wondering—as so many developing nations are wondering today—how to maintain its declared independence in an interdependent world. But James Madison's stuff—on the nature of politics, the countervailing of powers, the fencing in of factions, the separation of functions, the essence of governance—is strikingly timeless. He was describing a society in which, by deliberate design, nobody would be in general charge. It is a description, especially in "Federalist No. 10," well worth rereading today.

Durable ideas about executive leadership last much longer than two hundred years. One of the best books about what we now call "human resources management" was written in the third century A.D. by Liu Shao, a Chinese public administrator who hired out to manage principalities for local princes in the Middle Kingdom—a Niccolo Machiavelli of his time. Its chapter on how to conduct an interview can still be helpful in the twenty-first century.

Each of us has thus inherited an enormous body of wisdom about how to relate effectively to other people. When engineers invent a new gadget or scientists discover a new gene, you cannot even find its name in your favorite dictionary. But when you discover a workable way to bring people together in organizations to make a difference, you are more than likely to find it lucidly described in Lao-tzu's *Tao Te Ching,* Aristotle's writings, Bartlett's *Familiar Quotations,* or the Bible. Now that Mao Tse-tung is dead, literary archaeologists will doubtless unearth evidence that his most penetrating *Thoughts* were some ghostwriter's plagiarism from China's rich thesaurus of inherited practical wisdom.

So, as Walter Ong has written, "Time is in us: the material in our own bodies is five to ten billion years old . . . [and] the past is a massive fact in the sense of identity of every educated person today." A lively curiosity about that past is a primary qualification for leaders who would help mold our future identity.

What Matters?

In 1988 the University of Hawaii futurist James Dator returned from a visit to Australia with a poster advertising the prospect that the "greenhouse effect" might cause an irreversible rising of the world's oceans. The poster was large and mostly blue: it depicted the famous sails of the Sydney Opera House—the only things visible above the risen water. At the top of the poster, this legend:

If you act as though it matters and it doesn't matter, then it doesn't matter. But if you act as though it doesn't matter and it matters, then it matters.

What is it that matters, to those of us who respect the future? What matters is that the great transformations of our time are still driven by the inner logic of scientific discovery and technological innovation: the more we can discover, the better off we shall be.

Consider four concurrent science and technology revolutions, each in its uncaring ambivalence carrying fatal dangers and fateful opportunities for the human species.

Nuclear energy. A dimensional change in explosive power has created perils without precedent whether on purpose (Hiroshima, Nagasaki) or by mistake (Chernobyl). It has also created alternative sources of energy and additional tools for medicine. Yet by making it possible to invent weapons too powerful to use, science seems, by an accident of frightfulness, to have clamped a lid on the scale of violence—for the first time in world history.

The nuclear part of military strategy can now be best understood as a complex and expensive "information game" in which the military unusability of nuclear weapons enhances both lesser forms of violence and nonmilitary forms of power.

Biotechnology. Breakthroughs in deciphering the inherited information in our genes have provided us with a vast array of biotechnologies. Some of the applications are unimaginably frightful new capacities for genocide. But the same discoveries have also pointed to means of multiplying the productivity of plants and animals, ways to make protein cheap and abundant, to produce human insulin from bacteria, to manufacture more targetable antibiotics and vaccines against previously intractable diseases, even to correct birth defects in an individual fetus.

At a workshop of the World Academy of Art and Science in Hong Kong more than a decade ago, I listened to world-class experts as they speculated that biotechnology could (if we don't let ourselves be mesmerized by its dark potentials) be good news for "growth with fairness" worldwide.

The inherent nature of biological resources, and the fact that most of the world's rich supply of biomass—and most of the world's solar radiation, too—is concentrated in the so-called poorer parts of the world, holds promise that a world society focusing sharply on the constructive uses of the bioresource can be a fairer world.

Climate change. Atmospheric gases, products of industrial civilization, are now agents of large-scale, unprecedented change in the global climate. This global change could double back on human civilization, radically redistributing moisture and, in the span of a single lifetime, inundating not only Sydney but most of the world's great seaports. For the first time in world history we, *Homo sapiens,* the self-proclaimed wisest of all species, are able to do more to our natural environment than nature does to, and for, us.

But . . . the prospect of global environmental damage, the product of past breakthroughs in science and technology, is also generating new breakthroughs in thinking about global cooperation to avoid the damage. Shared environments such as outer space, the atmosphere, the deep oceans, and (so far) Antarctica can be neither owned nor divided; they constitute a natural global commons. Unlike the classic commons, where excessive use (an overpopulation of sheep) led to "enclosure," the tragedy of the global commons would be its competitive mismanagement, so littering it with waste, debris, and chemicals that, still undivided and unenclosed, it is rendered unusable for human purposes. The cooperative governance of the global commons is one of the great tasks of international statesmanship for the generation just ahead.

The informatization of society. Above all, the convergence of two separate lines of science and technology—faster computers and more reliable telecommunications—is creating societies where the dominant resource is information, the dominant activity no longer the production and exchange of things but the production and sharing of symbols.

Shortly before her death in 1946, Gertrude Stein, reaching for aphorisms even in her decline, complained that "Everybody gets so much information all day long that they lose their common sense." To regain our common sense, the informatization of society requires us to rethink the very fundaments of our philosophy—rethink an economics in which value inheres in scarcity, rethink laws based on ownership, rethink leadership based on hierarchy.

The good new news is that information, our newly dominant resource, is so clearly more accessible to more and more people that the spread of knowledge is rapidly eroding the power that once accrued to the few who were "in the know"—and thus changing for the better the global prospects for fairness.

A Future That Works

In futures studies, gloomy preoccupation with what might go wrong can paralyze action that's needed right now. Rosy sentimentality can also induce paralysis, that of Pollyanna: We'll surely manage to get out of the rut we're in, so why should I help push?

What's left is the role of practical visionary, dedicated to steer-ing us through the deep but narrow channel that divides Pollyanna from Cassandra. This is the world's highest calling—and a function paradoxical enough to have appealed to that master of paradox, Lao-tzu. ("If the sage would guide the people, he must serve with humility. If he would lead them, he must follow behind," *Tao Te Ching*, #66.)

One practical visionary, the Norwegian explorer Thor Heyer-dahl, told me that he had edited his philosophy down to seven words: *"Translate ideas into events, to serve people."* The starting point for thought-leading-to-action is the imaging of a future that works. And that's where the leader as futurist comes in.

Commentary on Chapter Ten

When I found that my career was on alternating current, swinging back and forth between public service and academic administration, I ruminated a good deal about the contrasts in the dynamics of getting things done in different kinds of organizations. As I tried to place all organizations along a spectrum from the most vertical to the most horizontal, it was easy to see that universities, hospitals, and scientific laboratories favored more consultation, suasion, and consensus, while military organizations, businesses, and government agencies were described with charts that looked like pyramids, with recommendations going up and orders coming down.

But I noticed that while top executives looked as though they held vast power in their hands, they themselves seemed more impressed with the difficulty of getting things done—and spent most of their time in essentially lateral consultations. I came to understand a comment attributed to the Czar Nicholas. "I do not rule Russia," he said at a moment of frustration. "Ten thousand clerks do."

This is what led me to speculate, in a book *(The Future Executive)* published thirty years ago, that "accelerating growth in the size and complexity of organization systems seems destined to move *the whole spectrum* away from the more formal, hierarchical, order-giving styles of doing business and toward the more informal, fluid workways of bargaining, brokerage, advice and consent."

That trend is more obvious in 2002 than it was in 1972. But I thought it might still be useful to include in this collection of essays a very early effort, only slightly updated from its first appearance in *Public Administration Review* in 1960, to describe the future of leadership from my then angle of vision, as an academic dean. Its description of the horizontal terrain doesn't seem to have withered with age.

10

The Dean's Dilemma
Leadership of Equals

At Parris Island, South Carolina, on April 8, 1956, Staff
Sergeant Matthew C. McKeon—a Marine drill instructor—
barked an order to a platoon of recruits, and they promptly marched
into water over their heads. Since some of them couldn't swim, they
drowned. A few must have reflected on that possibility ahead of
time. But published reports of the ensuing investigation failed to
reveal that any of the recruits considered disobedience as an option.

That Parris Island platoon can stand as the limiting case of vertical administration, in which a maximum of authority has been delegated upward to the issuers of orders by those who subsequently
receive them. Somewhere near the other end of the long and colorful spectrum of administration, you will find an academic dean
working with a faculty. Here members of the platoon have refrained
from delegating much of their hard-won authority to the sergeant;
they expect the dean neither to drill nor to instruct. In the academic world, the premium is not on collective orderliness, as at Parris Island, but on cheerful orneriness, as at Harvard.

Examples can doubtless be found of even more extreme forms of
horizontalness in managing human affairs. The resistance of physicians to order and conformity is also legendary, though the financial
regularities of Medicare and insurance companies have latterly
brought medical doctors into something of a corral. But an academic

faculty certainly is irregular enough to invalidate much of the hierarchical imagery that served for too long as general theory in public administration and business management.

My effort here will be to set down some personal observations on the role of deans as middle management in academia. The word *management*, with its heavy connotation of efficiency and good order, applies dubiously, if at all, to academic administration. But there is no question about the other word. The dean is by definition in the middle. It is a not unattractive place to be: the academic dean has more contact with the substance of education than the university's president and trustees, and affects the allocation of more resources than its full-time teachers and scholars.

Executive in a Legislative Environment

The mythology about deans is clear enough. On every university campus a whole genre of humor on the subject is transmitted in song and story from generation to generation. The newly appointed dean can confidently expect several dozen people to explain, ha-ha, that the definition of a dean is a mouse trying to act like a rat—or, in the purer corners of the humanities division, *as* a rat. Within a college or university faculty, the accepted hierarchy of values is best expressed by the description of a dean as not intelligent enough to be a professor and too intelligent to be a president.

Thus in faculty folklore, administration is the lowest form of subprofessional endeavor on the campus. Naturally it lacks the intellectual quality of teaching and book writing, but it lacks, too, the sense of artisanry (the "thingness," a philosophy professor might say) that lends a certain dignity to the work of janitors, the campus police, the food service, and the buildings-and-grounds crews. The administrators create nothing, initiate nothing; they exist to serve the teachers and scholars—and since they keep forgetting that this is their primary role they must be periodically reminded of it by exquisitely worded shafts of faculty wit.

This mythology is of course an indispensable element in the dynamics of a college or university. It explains the otherwise inexplicable: that administrators by and large get higher salaries, ampler work space, larger travel budgets, and more office help than the other members of the academic family. Teaching and scholarship are the purpose of the enterprise; how else can this favored treatment be justified but as the distressingly materialistic inducement required to make sure somebody will step forward to perform the paper-pushing tasks whose marginality to the real business of education is expressed in the pejorative term *overhead?*

The difficulty most people have in understanding academic administration is that they hear it described with words and concepts borrowed from hierarchical structures. But academic administration is in its important essentials a legislative process. The faculty, like a body of legislators, is plural. To draw a proper organization chart, you would need to use a roll of paper long enough to spread all the faculty members out on it horizontally. The dean is at best a majority leader with access to significant forms of patronage; on some issues, the dean may have to settle for acting as leader of the minority.

(This metaphor for an academic organization chart has to be used with an eye for unintended consequences. When I was president of the University of Hawaii, I spoke in this vein at a meeting where several newspaper reporters were present. One of them reported that I had used a roll of toilet tissue as my metaphor; the resulting flap was not serious, but it lasted a day or two.)

The essential characteristic of academic life is thus a fierce conviction that each of its participants is in important senses free and equal, empowered to decide within wide limits both the content of scholarship and the allocation of teaching loads. Some of the members, to be sure, are more equal than others. But power does not ride with position to the extent that it typically does in a government bureau or a corporate enterprise. The influence of the individual faculty member is paradoxically compounded of long tenure with a single institution plus the known ability to move elsewhere at the drop of a hat.

Outside Repute and Inside Influence

To illuminate the stage on which the dean (and to some extent the department chair as well) must play a peculiar role, it may be useful to compare the dynamics of hierarchical bureaucracies with what happens in an academic faculty.

If in a hierarchical organization you place on the table a new function that the organization must perform, you can count on a more or less polite struggle developing as to who will handle it. The success of each unit chief is measured by the progressive enlargement of that unit's responsibilities. Fully two decades before Parkinson's law was proclaimed, Chester Barnard argued that an organization's survival and growth were the only valid criteria by which the organization can be judged—or, indeed, can judge itself. By aggrandizing itself, each unit of a hierarchical system helps aggrandize the system as a whole. Charles E. Wilson was in the main intellectual stream when, on the assumption that General Motors was part of the United States, he implied in his famous "vice versa" that what was good for the part was good for the whole.

Not necessarily so in the administration of an academic faculty. Place a new function on the table at a faculty meeting and you are well on your way to losing your audience entirely. The dynamics of a faculty are centrifugal, not centripetal.

The reason is not far to seek. The careers of the scholar-teachers on the faculty do not depend *primarily* on their position in the power structure of their own institution, but on their individual repute in their own fields of specialization. The research chemist will get to the top of that profession through chemical research, not by sitting on university committees to work out a freshman general-education program in the arts and sciences. It is more relevant to an anthropologist's career to fathom the tribal symbolism of a remote village than to study the equally curious mythology of a modern college. The scholar who is trying to decide whether Shakespeare was really a reactionary in the midst of the Protestant Reformation can hardly be bothered to spend an evening a week representing an abstraction called "the humanities" on a university-wide committee on long-range building plans.

The professors' primary life is therefore lived in a variety of professional fields. The basis for their self-esteem, a mirror of the esteem of others they admire, comes largely from outside the formal structure that hires and pays—but often cannot fire—them. The fact that students, not to mention janitors and townspeople, regard them as savants and call them *doctor*—this they are likely to take for granted. It is the friendship and professional regard of colleagues in their own department and similar departments across the nation and abroad that they covet most—because it is the hardest to come by. For it is members of that community who have some reason for an informed opinion: they see the journal articles and may even read the books.

Even influence within the academic structure depends ultimately on professors' regional or national repute in their own professional fields. As colleagues and administrators move about at educational conventions and intellectual soirees, they will develop greater and greater esteem for those whose names are mentioned with approval and admiration. By the same token, those who seem unknown or regarded by professional peers as superficial or passé will find themselves passed over by the people who regulate travel funds, control faculty loads, decide who shouldn't be bothered with teaching the

8 A.M. classes, and determine which faculty offices will be supplied with new bookcases.

When it comes to salary, professors' bargaining power on the inside is directly correlated with their marketability on the outside. Nothing is so helpful to a dean trying to get someone a raise as the ability to say the university will lose the professor if an outside offer is not matched. One or two competitive offers a year, carefully leaked to the rumor network in time to influence next year's academic budget, will keep the salary escalator working satisfactorily, without all the trouble of actually packing up and moving somewhere else.

The dependence of professors on outside rather than internal repute also helps explain another fact that both baffles and pleases the new academic administrator. In a hierarchical organization, candid communication is often difficult because people are wary and overpolite about each other. People in bureaucracies, public or private, know by instinct that "the less I say about X, the less X is likely to say about me." In a government agency or business firm, blocks to internal communication are often a major management puzzle. Not so in an academic faculty. From the very moment of assuming office, the dean will find a disarming and sometimes jarring internal frankness on the part of those faculty members who are secure in their external reputations.

Leader in Search of Consensus

The external repute of individuals is only half of faculty dynamics. It is the controlling factor in the individual's position as a claimant on the college or university's resources and its administrators' goodwill. But it does not determine the individual professor's position in that oligarchical power structure for which *faculty democracy* is the favored euphemism.

Despite the growth of administrative overhead in colleges and universities, every faculty manages to retain for itself some real power to make, or veto, important decisions. The list typically includes promotions (especially as to academic rank), research leaves and other services to the faculty, revisions of the curriculum, approval of degrees including the honorary variety, and legislation about the conditions of academic freedom. In the structure of influence to handle such matters as these, professors' national distinction as scholars or widespread repute as lively teachers are by no means the major portion of this segment of their ticket of admission to the elite. Personal effectiveness and skill in negotiation are perhaps the most important factors. But seniority and long tenure also count for much.

As in other legislative processes, the rule of seniority is combined with a periodic popularity contest to select the elite corps of perennial surrogates for the masses. (The dean, as "majority leader," is also normally appointed by and with the advice and consent of the faculty.) To qualify for continuing leadership, the members of the faculty elite have to be sharp, tough, and honest, people with suasive skills, approachable personalities, and a bent toward consensus rather than command and control. These are the kinds of people you would expect to survive in legislative leadership—and will be increasingly in demand in executive leadership as *uncentralization* becomes more and more the way to manage complexity.

The resulting aristocracy of tenure manages the elective committees, and the same opinion-leaders are naturally selected by the administration for appointive posts to serve as conduits to the faculty at large. As in other parts of our social complexity, the leaders who serve on committees are expected to complain vigorously about the proliferation of committees and the administrative burdens they have to carry.

A committee can of course make collective decisions only on matters that do not contravene the vital interests of any wakeful member. In academic committees the members' normal posture will be complaisant apathy until something vital to their own department or discipline comes up; professorial courtesy is as strong a tradition at the monthly faculty meeting as senatorial courtesy is on Capitol Hill. Thus the only curriculum revisions that don't breeze through the faculty screens erected to "maintain standards" are those that raise jurisdictional issues: the eyebrows of the sleepiest economist will twitch when the engineering school brings up "economics for engineers." But generally no questions are asked; no one wants to be identified as a carping critic in someone else's field, as that inevitably exposes the asker's next proposals to withering cross-fire.

The review of curriculum through faculty committees is unlikely to be very illuminating anyway. Every academic dean soon learns the standard ploy, which is to pour new wine in old bottles. If a new faculty member wants to teach a new course, the old-timers in any established institution can, with a little research, exhume an approved course number and description to serve as a suitable vessel for the new material.

Experienced faculty members practice the familiar arts of legislation, notably log-rolling: "you approve the promotion of my young colleague and I'll approve the promotion of yours." They sometimes tend toward policies strikingly similar to those of the old craft unions, which may help explain why in so many colleges and universities, faculty members have opted to be represented by unions.

When faculty groups, however organized, discuss their own salaries—which they do frequently with well-justified anguish—the net result is usually not to propose increasing the salaries of the profoundest scholars, the most inspiring teachers, and the most externally marketable stars; efforts are often focused on raising the minimum wage for each professorial grade. The unhappy result is to skew the incentive system in a manner that hardly persuades the best teachers to stay and the weaker ones to look for some other line of work.

"Faculty democracy" implies a system of voting by majority rule. But a better description of how it works might be the Javanese tradition of *gotong-royong*. In Java's villages, and indeed in most non-Western cultures, the leaders talk things out until those who really care how it comes out agree on a course of action—an outcome supported by the apathy of those who don't care. Something like this happens in a Quaker meeting, or in our own jury system—and, in practice, in most collective decision making where the leaders are wise enough to avoid votes that simply take snapshots of what's not yet agreed, and reserve voting only to record formally a consensus already achieved by informal, sometimes tedious, bargaining and compromise.

Fluid Drive

The academic dean's central function can thus be described as the deferential manipulation of an essentially legislative process. This requires a maximum of apparent referendum and a minimum of overt initiative on the dean's part. Just as a legislator can gain a point by associating a favored cause with the rights of legislatures generally, so a faculty member always has in reserve one debating point of devastating potency: "We disagree with the dean about this. Shouldn't we show the administration that the faculty can't be dictated to?" Most groups, on or off campus, will not regard any idea as acceptable unless it is considered as partly the product of the group's initiative. Academic faculties are no exception to this natural law of human relations.

The dean not only works with the faculty but represents it in arguments with the president—or, in large institutions, with that vague, oblong, undifferentiated entity known as "the central administration" or "the front office." In this relationship the dean will find little nourishment in the principles of scientific management.

In managing financial affairs, for example, deans should avoid being taken in by scholarly writings about the virtues of central budgeting. As the ones in the middle, deans have influence directly proportional to their ability to scrounge resources beyond the university budget that can be diverted to faculty purposes—salary supplements, research grants, travel opportunities, consulting jobs, summer workshops, and the like. Fitness to participate in a complicated budgetary shell game is part of every dean's job description.

Flexibility is to be found in the opposite of central budgeting— a large number of budgetary bird-baths, representing a wide variety of financial sources, intermingled in the most complex possible manner. The goal of excessive complexity is all too easily reached. At the Maxwell School of Citizenship, I thought I had reached *nirvana* when it was clear that no one, either in the faculty or the central administration, could remember all of the twenty-three separate sources of the school's financial support—except, of course, my secretary and myself.

The rewards for survival in the jungle of academic administration are many. Professor James McCamy of the University of Wisconsin once remarked that professors are vowed to poverty and chastity in exchange for the freedom to eat lunch only with friends. For the middle managers, this freedom is somewhat more restricted unless their friends are all moneyed folk. Yet the dean's opportunity to live and work in the company of colleagues unashamed of their intellectuality; the stimulation of daily contact with bright young people and with campus life; the obligation to circulate in the off-campus world as a representative of and salesman for organized brainwork—these are great rewards. Few tasks in our society offer so much and provide a monthly paycheck too.

The price of this energetic and congenial work is the dean's willingness to learn that in the management of academic organizations the premium is on casual informality rather than rigid structure, on informal consensus rather than formal procedures for action. The administration of brainwork is advanced not by the rearrangement of solid particles but by chemical reactions in a liquid solution.

"If a man's thoughts are penetrating and his way fluid, while his plans are marvelously clever, such a one is called a strategist." So wrote Liu Shao in *The Study of Human Abilities* seventeen hundred years ago, during the politically chaotic period of the Three Kingdoms in China. He might have been setting up recruitment criteria for an academic dean. Few deans are penetrating thinkers and marvelously clever besides. But we all apprehend by instinct that Fluid Drive is the *Tao* of academic administration.

Commentary on Chapter Eleven

The spread of knowledge greatly influences the way people in modern organization systems work together—working *with* rather than *for* each other. An early effort to take a still picture of this moving target was for a book thirty years ago—*The Future Executive* (Harper & Row, 1972). Some of what was then an iffy forecast has meanwhile become the observable reality around us. This essay uses the same six "style" categories I found useful then, which I still find useful now, but it updates in all sorts of ways what is said about them.

11

A Style for Complexity

More Leadership of Equals

When a university starts looking for a new president, a government leader needs a new political executive, or a large private organization seeks an executive for a major assignment, some group of trustees or advisers or management consultants is often asked to write down the specifications for the person sought.

They find this deceptively easy to do. The trouble is, their list of desired qualities is likely to describe the Angel Gabriel. In the end they satisfy themselves that the paragon they really want is otherwise employed, so members of the search committee start belatedly to look for a fallible, flesh-and-blood human being.

If we now try, taking into account the new knowledge environment, to sketch a profile of the executive leaders we need, we risk tumbling into a similar trap. For one thing, the spread of knowledge keeps multiplying the number of people who serve in thousands of contexts as executive leaders. In the United States alone, a million Americans would be a very conservative estimate at the beginning of this new century.

It may be hard to believe that so many leaders can all be alike even in one respect, let alone in many. Yet if you look around at the people you would regard as leaders and focus on those you think are especially effective, you will find a striking similarity in certain qualities and points of style. For one thing, they all display the sheer physical energy needed to keep up with the job in an environment of extreme complexity. Beyond that, the executive leaders of the future will, I think, be marked by a set of attitudes and aptitudes that seem to be necessary for the leadership of equals, which is the key to the administration of complexity. They will be more intellectual, more reflective, than the executives of the past. They will be low-key people, with soft voices and high boiling points. They will show a talent for consensus and a tolerance for constructive ambiguity. They will have a penchant for unwarranted optimism. And they will find private joy in complexity and change.

Physical Energy

The most obvious of these is physical energy. Leadership tasks typically involve long hours and much homework. The broader the responsibility, the harder it is to leave it at the office. The person who has decided to point the way or take the lead is seldom able to say that the next step is finished and is therefore not to be worried about anymore.

Dr. Mottram Torre, who brooded for years about the dangers of psychiatric disability in high office, listed three common characteristics of "high energy level personalities": a significant skill in channeling energy, the ability to conserve energy by getting others to share in the making of decisions, and the ability to release energy and relax.

Almost any physical or mental illness diminishes vitality and heightens self-concern. For an executive leader, serious illness results in a lowered interest in the work to be done: a tendency to shut out new information (there is too much already), further analysis (the problems on the executive desk are already more complicated than the human spirit can bear), and uncomfortable peers (who likely will ask the executive to think some more, rather than decide on the basis of current knowledge and opinions).

In an environment of accelerating change and compounding complexity, such insulation from the new, the complicated, and the uncomfortable may cause the ill executive to pursue unsuccessful lines of action, which might have been different if the person most responsible were healthy, alert, and fully informed. Any large organization is witness to dozens of examples in the course of a year.

Our political history shows how crucial it can be for a public official to be feeling well at moments of destiny—Franklin Roosevelt's performance at Yalta ("He won't take any interest in what we are trying to do," Winston Churchill complained); Woodrow Wilson's tactical rigidity when he was bedridden yet still president; Abraham Lincoln's damaging hesitations during the first year of his presidency ("When hurried by the pressure of rapidly changing, uncontrollable circumstances and events, he tended to become . . . inwardly indecisive," says historian Edward J. Kempf).

Reflective Leadership

It used to be said that a good executive could always hire brains; other executive qualities were harder to come by. In *The Functions of the Executive*, published in 1938, Chester Barnard listed intelligence last, and it seemed reluctantly, among the talents required. There may still be training programs that teach executives to hire good people and delegate them full responsibility for clearly defined pieces of the work to be done. But modern complexity has rendered this conventional wisdom both unconventional and unwise.

The system executive is acutely aware that none of the pieces of the work can be clearly defined; most of them are not even clearly within the leader's jurisdiction. The wisest executives no longer ask for "completed staff work" on important matters. They know they have to immerse their own minds in the staff work, because it is in the staff work where most of the policy decisions are made.

The work of executives often consists in meeting a series of unforeseeable obstacles on the road to an objective that can be clearly specified only when they are close to reaching it. They try to imagine the unforeseen by posing contingencies and asking themselves how their organization systems would adjust if these chances arose. Of course the planned-for contingency never happens; something else happens instead. The planning therefore does not produce a usable plan but something more precious: people better trained to analyze the unpredicted and to winnow out for the decision makers (who are almost always plural) the choices that would be too costly to fudge or postpone.

This requires that the participating experts and staff assistants acquire some understanding of what it is like to be an executive leader, how it feels to frame a decision that will stick. But it also demands that the decision makers themselves participate in the staff work, try to understand the expert testimony, and measure the options and filter the imagined consequences of each through their best computers, which are their own brains.

Even in collective research, the breakthrough ideas usually turn out to be the product of one person's brooding, of one person's reading, of someone's sudden inspiration that fits together in a usable pattern the random data and partial reasoning of others—an idea honed in the darkest hours of the night by that marvelous instrument, the reflective human mind.

Anyone who has worked with organized systems has to be impressed with the capacity of the human brain to cope with complexity. Viewed as a sensitive computer not limited to quantified bits, the brain is able to take in a wide range of observations, weigh them according to their multiple relevance, store them in a memory of fantastic dimensions, retrieve them with high speed and reasonable accuracy, organize them into options, come up with a practical course of action, and transmit instructions to other parts of the body in a fraction of a second. Even so, an organization system is by definition too ramified for any one executive's mind to encompass. But the executive can comprehend the relations among its parts and its people, and can concentrate that energy on the parts that don't fit together—on the relationships that are not working well enough.

The executive leader must therefore be something of an intellectual, not just by training but by temperament as well. The executive who isn't personally plowing through the analysis and reflecting on what it means is not making decisions but merely presiding while others decide. The obligation to think hard, fast, and free is the one executive function that can neither be avoided nor delegated to others.

Soft Voice, Low Key

As executive leaders test their brains against their corners of the great complexity, they find that certain leadership workways work best. The hallmarks of this modern style are the soft voice and the low key.

The signs are already much in evidence. The manners of a dean toward faculty members in a good university are spreading in domains where standing at attention is still in living memory. Even near the more vertical end of the spectrum of administration, in infantry divisions, fighter squadrons, and warships at sea, the men who are running things find less and less need for a loud voice or a parade-ground manner. If they want to reach large numbers of people, they don't have to raise their voices; they order up an electronic amplifier. If they have orders to give to subordinates, they are more and more likely to call a meeting and act by consensus—or at least to formulate the command as a suggestion.

On a visit to Israel some years ago, I found this shifting style illustrated with the story of an Israeli battalion performing a drill in honor of a visiting dignitary. In a quiet conversational voice the captain gives the order: "Battalion march." The visitor, a senior general, is surprised, and leans over to give the young man a word of advice-from-experience. "You have to *shout* the order," he explains, "so they all start together." The captain smiles tolerantly at this advice from the age of administrative pyramids. "It's all right, sir," he replies. "The word will get around."

While working in Europe as ambassador to the North Atlantic Treaty Organization, I had occasion to visit a number of military posts related to the NATO defense system. It was hard to avoid the conclusion that a growing proportion of all the officers' time was spent dealing horizontally with people who were not "under" or "over" them. The infantry captain who calls in air support of a beleaguered company is not dealing up and down a hierarchy, but negotiating across several chains of command. The colonel designated as "base commander" may find representatives of fifteen or twenty different U.S. military organizations camping on the two square miles of the base. None of these units is part of the chain of command; they deal with the commander as contractual partners, the way a tenant deals with a landlord.

In the military as elsewhere, the more complicated things become, the more all the decision makers are consulting, bargaining, clearing with people they cannot order around and who cannot order them around. The changes in executive style that horizontalness makes mandatory brings military administration each day closer to the way hospitals, higher education, and scientific research have to be managed.

The more critical the function and the more split-second the timing, the more likely you are to find in charge individuals with a relaxed appearance who direct by indirection and confer the maximum personal responsibility on each staff member. I once sat above the flight deck of an aircraft carrier in the Mediterranean, watching the "air boss" at work. He was obviously depending heavily on the extemporaneous originality, the ability to adapt known procedures to unknown emergencies, of every sailor in the crew. He was responsible for planes being catapulted from the deck and safely landed on it, an intricate and dangerous operation. Yet the air boss infrequently gave an order; most of the time he was monitoring a complex but familiar procedure, intervening only when he saw trouble developing that the men running around on the deck couldn't see. Since the flight deck in use is a very noisy place, the key participants in its choreography are wired for sound. The air boss could hear what they said to each other, and that was how most of the work got done; he could preempt a decision, wave off an incoming plane, or call up reinforcements to handle a crisis. But the system wouldn't have worked at all if it had depended on cumbersome vertical recommendations and approvals. Each sailor involved was using personal judgment, sharpened by training to be sure, while the air boss watched, monitored, calculated, always thinking ahead—and felt no need to prove his virility by shouting, even in the presence of visitors.

The new style is actually a technological imperative. Down in the bowels of the aircraft carrier, there was a large, dimly lit room full of serious young men bent over radar screens that showed the position of all aircraft and surface vessels in the general vicinity. Around the wall were displayed masses of current data, from the names and locations of the nearest alternate landing fields to current calculations of how much jet fuel each plane aloft had remaining in its tanks. Information about the drama above decks was exchanged in quiet, unemotional tones. The lesson for executive style was plain: Complexity of operation magnified small errors and made the whole system vulnerable. People who got excited too easily were likely to get in the way, and had to simmer down regardless of rank.

The degree to which this new style has taken hold in the armed services varies greatly according to the function to be performed. A complicated planning assignment is much more likely to be handled in a collegial mode than the taking of a hill by a company of infantry. But with the spread of knowledge, even in the most vertical structures officers can no longer be quite as certain as their fathers might have been that an order automatically produces the consent to follow it. And some of their fathers will remember that, in Vietnam a generation ago, they assembled their platoons in seminars to discuss how to take that next hill—and why the war was worth fighting.

The Nature of Consensus

It is functional for an executive leader to be low-key because the unique executive function is to develop consensus around a subjective human purpose. As larger systems are organized to assess and control for human purposes the innovations of technology, the new systems will require of their managers an even more collegial, consensual style. And as this trend gains momentum, it will render obsolescent in executive process the decision-making procedure we in the Western world have considered the heart of democracy—choosing up two sides and voting.

Two-sidedness is built deep into American culture. We would experience a kind of culture shock if we saw more than two boxers in a ring, more than two teams on an athletic field, more than two sides in a collective bargaining session, more than two adversaries litigating in a courtroom, more than two parties in a legislature. Third parties are often excluded from the electoral debates that have become a mandatory feature of U. S. political campaigns. Yet in problem solving outside these artificial constructs there is almost no such thing as a two-sided problem. A two-sided analysis of the Arab-Israeli conflict, a corporate price rise, or an issue in university governance is a nonsense analysis.

For one week while I was in the State Department, I conducted an empirical test of two-sidedness: For every foreign policy issue that reached my desk, I asked myself how many different sides were interested and engaged. My notes at the end of that week hardly constitute a scientific finding, even if they carry the prestige of quantification: on the average, each of the issues I dealt with in Washington that week had 5.3 sides.

In a complex organization system, even the pretense of two-sidedness would be ridiculous. The executive leader proceeds by persuasion and consensus. It is instinctively obvious that an orderly two-sided debate on any important issue is bound to confuse consideration of a problem with five sides or more, and thus inhibit the process of bringing people together in large systems to make things happen. *Robert's Rules of Order* is at best useless in building the kinds of organizations required to tackle the greatest problems with which the executive leader has to deal. At worst, it is a reactionary bible for those whose subtle purpose is to divide communities and prevent community action.

Voting will remain useful for some purposes—to record the majority's will in a legislature when negotiation and compromise have failed to persuade a minority, and to elect the legislators and political executives who will serve as surrogates for the people's outrage and confusion. But as our problems mount, it is all too clear that more and more of them cannot be solved by bringing them to a vote. In the short run it may be necessary to outvote the polluters; but for the longer pull they need to be convinced that contributing to pollution is an act against their own interest. It is not enough to declare against the status quo. Change has to be organized in such a way as to include in the changes the devotees of things as they are. It is only a first step to choose sides for and against civil rights; we have to persuade those who, in pursuit of their own free convictions, would deny the freedom of conviction to others.

When I have visited the Pacific islands and cultures to the west of our so-called Western nation, I've noticed that Pacific and Asian friends seem instinctively to know what we who have grown up in the Western democracies find so hard to accept. It would not occur to most Chinese to hold a meeting at a rectangular table, forcing the participants to choose sides before they can even sit down. Despite their hierarchical form, the processes of Japanese business seem to leave lots of room for decisions by consensus. A Samoan board meeting, or a Javanese village council, somehow gets its business done without *Robert's Rules*. In much of the non-Western world, the decision making proceeds without ever choosing sides, in ways analogous to a jury or a Quaker meeting, through traditions that encourage men and women to talk out (or decide not to press) their differences—instead of hardening them by clarifying then voting on them.

The management of large organization systems requires a great deal of talking and listening in an effort to take every interest into account and yet emerge with relevant policy decisions and executive action. The world's work will not be tackled by identifying our differences but by sitting down, preferably at a round table, working hard at the politics of consensus, bringing people together rather than splitting them apart.

A central principle of consensus is that it is possible for people to agree on next steps to be taken if they carefully avoid trying to agree on *why* they are acting together. In a complex process each interested group may have a different reason for advocating action "in common cause." Typically, many of the actions desired can be concerted through negotiation—an executive leader normally serving as the orchestra conductor—provided no attempt is made to formulate a concerted philosophy, too.

Many years ago, at a meeting of Pacific Islanders, I came to understand a definition of consensus I have treasured and used ever since: *the acquiescence of those who care, supported by the apathy of those who don't.*

Unwarranted Optimism

Anyone with general executive experience has noticed that the most narrowly specialized staff member is likely to be the stubbornest staff holdout on what to do next. Gloom and reluctance are the hallmarks of expertise. That's why the executive leader must always be ready to supply a pinch of intuitive optimism to the stew of calculated costs and rationalized benefits.

Downbeat expertise has to be countered every day by leaders who insist on moving toward the human imperatives that lie beyond the specialized knowledge. Some readers will doubtless have had the same experience I have often faced: You're sitting at your desk with a semicircle of experts in front of you, trying to decide what to do next about some difficult problem. You ask each specialist, who knows everything there is to know about one corner of the great complexity, what we should do together to solve the larger puzzle we all know has to be solved. Then you aggregate the advice and it adds up to: "Do nothing, cautiously." At that point, someone in the room has to be willing to say, "Let's try it anyway," or "Let's take this first step, and see where it leads."

I first started focusing on the leader's upbeat function long ago, when the expert predictions of disaster centered on the alarming increase in world population and the degradation of the environment. (The U. S. population experts may have been compensating for past error: the Census Bureau in 1945 guessed that the United States would reach a population of 167 million by 1995, then we rocketed past that figure in the mid-1950s.) The dangers of overpopulation were very real, but they did not need to be embroidered with straight-line projections that depended for their validity on the assumption that the probable countervailing trends would not countervail. In the decades since then, it has turned out that education, economic development, contraception technologies, and changes in the status of women, all leading to the spread of democracy and the prospect of prosperity, are powerful counter-weights indeed.

The early environmentalists were likewise prone to play with long-range forecasts, in which the gloomiest of alternative futures emerged as the most probable. There is a contribution to be made by professional gloom, if it moves people-in-general to insist on changing the future by acting in the present. But it isn't prophecies of disaster that usually move people to action. A mayor has difficulty coalescing the urban electorate around a charge that there is no place to park downtown. Yet the mayor can often develop political and financial support for a plan to build municipal parking garages. What moves people to action is more hope than fear, not just a vision of how bad things might become but a vision of how things might be improved.

This is where the executive leader comes in. It is a professional obligation of the craft to supply the unwarranted optimism that sets the agent of action off from the well-documented advisory prophet of doom. A leader's contribution to any organization is to remember that the ethical content of planning need not be limited to a comparison in which the future seems less attractive than the present. As Teilhard de Chardin emphasized (perhaps this is the reason for his latter-day popularity), people are not to be passive witnesses but participants in the evolutionary process.

If planning is improvisation on a general sense of direction, then the executive leaders' primary task is to establish, maintain, advertise, and continuously amend a sense of direction that their colleagues in complexity can share. The conviction that the goals they help set are possible of achievement is an indispensable part of their psyches. Theirs is the optimism of the doer. It may be unwarranted by the experience of others, but it is justified by their own determination to organize a future with a difference.

Ralph Waldo Emerson said it, long ago: "Nothing great was ever achieved without enthusiasm."

The Exhilaration of Choice

Executive leaders of the future will have to be healthy, brainy, low-key, collegial, optimistic, and one thing more: they will need to positively enjoy complexity and constant change.

People who shy away from executive work often say they feel imprisoned by the multiplicity of options and the ambiguities of jurisdiction that are the stuff of large-scale organization. Effective executives, by contrast, turn out to be folks who delight in the chance to choose the best path according to their own lights. For the executive leader, the feel of administration is the exhilaration of choice.

At Expo 67 in Montreal, the tasteful exhibit from Czechoslovakia attracted the most attention, and its outstanding feature was a film about the selection of options in motion. The film was remarkable for its time; it engaged the audience in ways that producers of interactive experiences for TV and the Web—even with more sophisticated technologies at their disposal—only caught up with decades later.

The screenplay started conventionally enough: The day is warm; a beautiful girl, scantily clad, is ironing in her apartment. By some series of accidents I cannot remember, she goes out into the hall wearing nothing but a towel, and the door slams behind her. Of course she doesn't have her key, and she is distraught as she imagines her iron, still on, burning the fabric and setting the apartment house afire. She knocks on the door of the apartment next door; a man emerges. He, too, has a problem: his wife has gone out for a moment. Should he invite the nearly naked girl into his apartment while he tries to help her?

Suddenly the movie stops, the house lights go on, and a real-life man appears through a trap door on the stage in front of the darkened screen. The man is the actor we have just been watching on the screen. "Stop the movie!" he cries, and turns to the audience. "What shall I do now?" He explains that each member of the audience has a console in the arm of the theater seat; each of us can vote whether he should invite the toweled blonde into his apartment or shut the door in her face. The audience votes, chivalry wins by a narrow margin, the house lights go off and the movie reappears, pursuing the action that follows from the option we have selected.

The wife then returns, draws the too-obvious conclusion, and leaves her man. There is still an iron presumably setting the whole building on fire, and it is not long before another excruciating choice presents itself. Again the movie stops, the trap door opens, the girl actress this time appears in the flesh (though properly clothed according to Eastern European standards) and asks the audience for a decision. The screenwriter evidently had a whole scenario worked out for each option, no matter which fork in the road each audience selected each time the movie was shown. After a hilarious hour, with more audience participation than I have ever seen in a movie house, the ambiguities were resolved in an ironic O. Henry finish.

The enormous popularity of this 1967 film is easily explained: the ethical dilemmas it presented were transmuted from a celluloid image to the reasoning conscience of each member of the audience. Instead of observing other people's dilemmas, their choices suddenly became ours.

The central function of executive leaders is to choose among alternative action options as they go along—not just for themselves but for others, too. The more responsibility they carry, the harder the dilemmas they face. Indeed, only the difficult-to-resolve issues ever reach them for resolution.

When I worked in Washington it was hard not to notice that by the time an issue gets to the ultimate political executives, it has proved insoluble by logic and reason. The chief ingredients in "high policy" seemed to be gut feelings and ethical hunch. Robert McNamara, who as Secretary of Defense and president of the World

Bank tried so hard to apply reason to policy, concluded that "Management is, in the end, the most creative of all the arts, for its medium is human talent itself."

Like painting or sculpture or dance, the management of social complexity cannot be taught by rote, but it *can* be learned by example and inspiration and unremitting practice. What Michel de Montaigne said of the arts and sciences is doubly true of the qualities of executive leadership: they are not cast in a mold, but are formed and perfected by degrees, by frequent handling and polishing, as bears leisurely lick their cubs into form.

The Joy of Motion

What makes executives' lives especially exciting is that the choices they make, or help make, are *in motion*. It used to be said that the good executive was driving; the more accurate word would now be *steering*. The momentum is already built in—the executive's task is to give it direction, to cause the momentum to serve a subjective human purpose by channeling it in a system managed by human beings and not by blind fate.

Because I used to race sailboats in my youth, I have often thought the feel of executive responsibility analogous to the feel of a small sailboat in competition. If I'm the skipper, I must know just what my craft will and won't do, and what my crew can handle, especially in emergencies. I must have done my homework—looked up the timing and force and direction of the tides and currents that afternoon, listened to the latest weather forecasts, studied wind-shift tactics and the racing rules. I also have to know as much as possible about the psychology of the other skippers and the performance of their boats—some faster in light airs, some able to point higher on a windward beat, some especially swift on a spinnaker run. With all these data stored for instant retrieval, I must analyze a constantly moving situation, in which the air, the water, the other boats, and my own boat are continuously changing relations to one another. And then I have to make decisions—several major policy decisions per minute if the class is large and the competition keen. Win or lose, I'm unlikely to be bored.

A year after the British electorate had retired him as Chancellor of the Exchequer in a Labour Government, Roy Jenkins proposed skiing as the best way to describe the exhilaration of choice in motion. He contrasted private writing and public responsibility:

> A hard period of writing is like a walk up a steep mountainside. There is no natural momentum behind one. It all has to be self-generated. . . . [But the writer] can mostly control his own pace, and his intermediate failures are private rather than public. There are no onlookers to mock his periods of ineffective immobility.
>
> Ministerial work, on the other hand, is much more like skiing down a slalom course. The momentum is all on one's side, provided it can be controlled. There is little difficulty about generating the will to proceed. There is a rapid and relentless movement from one event to another . . . each event comes up with such rapidity that there is relatively little danger of falling through hesitation or over-anxiety. They have to be taken as they come, on the run; and a lot of things are better done this way.

Neither metaphor is very close. The object of executive work is not usually to win a race but to make cooperation work. And the slalom image would be better if at each gate the skier were presented with two or three alternative ways to proceed. But both images convey the essential sense of motion. Because the whole environment of administration is constantly in motion, nobody can quite know just how the situation looks to an individual executive leader except that person. Within the limits of relevance, therefore, the leader must choose a path and live with the consequences.

To some, the obligation to choose too fast and too often will seem a burden, a cause for complaint and a reason for frustration. But to those who have the stuff to be executive leaders, the momentum will carry its own excitement, and the opportunity to participate in destiny decisions will more than repay the days of committee-sitting and the nights of reading, writing, and thinking ahead.

Internalizing Credit

For many executive leaders, perhaps most, the exhilaration of choice is the primary reward for service and the chief ingredient in morale. But most of that feeling of joy in getting things done by getting decisions made has to be generated from within. To maximize personal morale, the executive leader has to learn to internalize credit for what gets done.

For a few executives, especially those in top positions, public notice and even approbation are available as inducements to develop the skills and carry the ethical burdens that go with their function in society.

There is of course the offsetting risk of public opprobrium. For a time, a new recruit to the ranks of executive leadership may feel that the choices to be made are so complicated, and the criteria of success so obscure, that it is almost impossible for outsiders to judge the executive's performance on the job. The probability is indeed diminishing of any interested public's being able to understand what the decision was about or what a particular executive's part in it was. Yet this does not necessarily make life safer for the executive leader. For when a judgment *is* rendered, the public's ignorance, combined with its ultimate power, may render the verdict more unfair than it might have been in simpler times or more static societies.

For most executive leaders, their very function precludes their taking credit for the most important things they do. The official who writes a policy speech for the President; the financial analyst whose staff work enables the boss to keep the firm in the black; the personnel manager who keeps a crack designer from quitting in disgust, and thus ensures better design work on next year's car; the general counsel who drafts a major piece of legislation, of which the senator who introduces it is said to be the "author"; the American ambassador who thinks up a useful initiative and then persuades a non-American colleague to float it publicly—none of these can take credit for their work without interfering with the desired results.

A good colleague doesn't hog the credit for collective accomplishment. And the mark of a good staff assistant is that the person functionally responsible for a decision not be deprived of the credit for making it.

When I managed a bureau in the State Department, served as a diplomatic mission chief at NATO, and later was chief executive of a state university system, I signed or uttered hundreds of memos, policy cables, speeches, and articles that were mostly the work of others. Editing them so that they sounded more like me, then acting as though they *were* mine, made them mine. Neither accolades nor backlash from supervisors or affected publics fell out on my advisers or ghostwriters. I was often fulsome in my private praise. But the colleagues who helped write my stuff had to learn the art of taking credit vicariously—and anonymously.

On several occasions in the 1960s, I contributed major chunks of thinking and writing to statements and foreign-policy speeches that historians correctly attribute to President John F. Kennedy, President Lyndon B. Johnson, Vice President Hubert H. Humphrey, and other luminaries of that yeasty decade. In the nature of things, the Kennedy biographer who had served as the President's chief writer was reluctant to attribute to others ideas originating here and there in the federal bureaucracy; those ideas became his as he formulated them with his antiphonal elegance. The President did not live to say what he himself remembered, but it is altogether probable that he thought the ideas in his policy speeches were his own. Wherever originated, he had made them his own by understanding them, editing them, and taking public responsibility for making them Presidential policy.

An Acquired Skill

The power of that final editing was borne in on me when, during the early 1960s, I worked as one of several people Adlai Stevenson depended on to draft official statements and public speeches. Stevenson was already a personality of world renown when he became President Kennedy's ambassador to the United Nations. In that position he was constantly on stage, and the relevant publics— including hundreds of diplomats from countries around the globe— parsed his every phrase as a clue to what the U.S government was going to do next.

His ghostwriters knew each other, of course; some, like the British economist Barbara Ward and the American historian Arthur Schlesinger Jr., were already well-known writers in their own right. We often consulted each other—especially when our loquacious friend asked two or more of us to draft the same upcoming speech.

Adlai Stevenson was well known as an eloquent speaker and an elegant writer; what most people didn't know was that he hated to start with a blank sheet of paper. It was a challenge to meet his rhetorical standard, and I never quite did. It was a source of humbling surprise and renewed admiration whenever he wielded his editorial pencil and enlivened some prose I had thought would be hard to improve. (That didn't always happen at his office desk. I vividly remember him sitting at head tables at formal dinner parties, still editing his speech while preliminary speakers were at the podium.)

But of course I knew that whatever he said, it was he who would be quoted and criticized—and judged by the White House, the Congress, the editorial writers, and the talking heads on radio and television. It obviously served no purpose for his scribes to highlight publicly the parts of his speeches they had written. I quickly learned that, for the ghostwriter, pride of authorship tastes better when it's instantly swallowed.

President Kennedy was acutely conscious of where credit and blame might fall. On one occasion, after we had contrived in his office a complicated scheme for handling some foreign-policy issue, he sent us back to Foggy Bottom with a cheerful parting shot. "I hope this plan works," said a smiling President of the United States. "If it does, it will be another White House success. If it doesn't, it will be another State Department failure." But I was in the Cabinet Room the day it became clear that the Bay of Pigs invasion was a fiasco; President Kennedy promptly took full responsibility for the mistake.

There are many kinds of social rewards for executive work short of applause from the general public. Usually a few people know the situation well, and their private encomiums count for much. The Central Intelligence Agency operatives or the FBI undercover agents, who may not even be able to tell their spouses what they are really doing, know that people in their own organization whose opinion they value are aware of their assignments and recording their triumphs.

Even in less secret parts of the government, and in business and the nonprofit sector too, most of the credit for accomplishment—and most of the blame for failure, too—has to be internalized. If what you are doing is useful, important, or subject to external criticism, many people will be glad to take credit for anything that works, that is done right—even if you think you did it all by yourself. Sharing the credit is costly only to your own ego; for the larger system you're serving, it's always a win-win game.

I learned in the diplomatic service to derive active pleasure from reflecting on my part in defusing several peace-and-security crises and averting a couple of near-wars, without boasting to anyone outside my immediate family.

The capacity to internalize the credit for what you do is certainly an acquired skill, unnatural to the human psyche. An executive leader needs to acquire it early, for the nature of modern leadership is that it doesn't show—and especially that it doesn't show off.

Commentary on Chapter Twelve

Just before I came back into government with the Kennedy administration early in 1961, I had been deaning and teaching public administration at the Maxwell School of Citizenship and Public Affairs, Syracuse University. One segment of the Executive Leadership course I offered was devoted to "public ethics." When I returned to government, I naturally kept on thinking about how to make sure I was behaving ethically. And I collected cautionary tales to illustrate the principles that were becoming clearer to me in action than they had been in the classroom.

When in 1969 I left government again and returned to academia, I felt ready to write my first book about executive leadership, which was published by Harper & Row in 1972 under the title *The Future Executive*. Some of what appears here was first drafted for the ethics chapter of that book. Reading this essay now, remember that some of it was written thirty years ago, in 1971. Most of the stories and characters may read like ancient history—depending on how old you are. But they were part of what led me to this way of thinking about public ethics, which I believe may be even more valid in the new century.

A note about vocabulary: That 1972 book was addressed to and written about people I called the Public Executives: leaders in every kind of organization who have responsibilities affecting the public interest—whether they are employed by a business enterprise, a nonprofit institution, or a government agency. (I have worked in all three sectors, but always considered myself a Public Executive as defined here.)

12

"The Very Definition of Integrity"

If you would not be known to do anything,
never do it.

—*Ralph Waldo Emerson*

During the time when Charles Van Doren was pretending to be an intellectual giant on a rigged TV quiz show, and before he was caught in the act, he and his legitimately famous father, Mark Van Doren, were chosen as "the Father-and-Son Team of the Year" by the National Father's Day Committee. The grateful remarks that father and son made in accepting the award, read through the hindsight of Charles's later confession that his brilliance was a hoax, take on the quality of prophetic wisdom.

Father was the first to speak. Our later knowledge leaves his words untarnished:

> I claim no credit for [Charles's] being what he is . . . people make their own intellectual and moral characters. If he was helped in making his by me . . . it was he who decided to accept the help. The decision in such matters is finally with ourselves. To say that responsibility begins at home should mean, I think, that it begins—and ends, too—in the individual. Sooner or later he must help himself. There are no alibis.

Charles Van Doren then rose to accept his public's accolade, and in the course of his remarks he spoke of his father:

> He has been able to move me, to laughter and to tears, for as long as I can remember. Both in public and in private—and that's of the greatest importance. For my father has been, to me, both a public and a private man. Oh, perhaps not as public a man as I have become recently. We have laughed about this, he and I. . . . But my experience has reminded me of something that he taught me—not consciously, I'm sure, but as an example. For the extraordinary thing about my father is that his public face and his private face have been the same. He has been the same man to the world as he has been to his family. And that is harder than it sounds. It is the very definition of integrity, I suppose.

Ethical Judgments Are Personal

I have argued elsewhere that a line cannot be drawn between public and private on the basis of ownership but only on the basis of interest and utility and purpose. It follows that the Public Executive is marked not by *affiliation* with a public agency but by *acceptance* of the public responsibility of the job, whatever the character of the organization in which it is being done.

And if the ultimate judgment about the quality of an executive's public actions can be made only by people-in-general, the ultimate court is the public's outrage. Therefore the best way to keep the Public Executives' feet to the fire is to make sure that the decisions in which they participate, and the identity of the participants, are publicly known. The best antidote to irresponsibility is openness.

This is a hard doctrine. It means that the quality of public ethics in our time and place rests in the first instance on the moral sensitivity, the political antennae, and the internalized standards of hundreds of thousands of Public Executives in thousands of public and apparently private organizations.

Each individual's conscience is already subject to a wide assortment of tugs and pulls—family ties, loyalty to many organizations (neighborhood, church, commune, volunteer agencies, schools, professional associations, as well as "the job"), professional ethics, personal ambition, personal health, and personal convictions about lifestyles. Now we add to this already complex moral burden an elusive responsibility to an often apathetic general public. And we say that in modern society the public interest must be first defined for each person by that person, for each situation in that situation.

The concept of the public interest has been analyzed so much by writers and teachers that I am reluctant to add another page to the literature. But I observe that in facing practical problems many people still think there must be some formula, some overriding principle, some universal criterion of judgment and action that is objective and ascertainable: "Didn't he *know* that what he did was against the public interest?"

Yet there is no ethical realm, let alone any book about ethics, from which the individual faced with complex judgments can pluck the answers to the questions that press in from all sides. And paradoxically, the more complex things become, the more personal the ethical judgments have to be. Cultural pluralism, diffusion of power, and horizontalness of decision making require us to think of the public interest not as a code of ethics for the world, or for the nation, or even for a single organization, but as a nontransferable way of thinking developed by individual Public Executives for their own use.

In practice this way of thinking is compounded of the perceived standards of others, molded to fit one's own experience in trying to apply those standards to real-life problems. We start by deriving our deep-down feelings about public responsibility from our early environment—from family and school and religion, from the organizations with which we are perforce associated, from heroes and friends and villains and enemies. Then as we gain more experience, we develop our personal notions from the injustices we see practiced or find we are practicing ourselves, from the examples we see of social and antisocial behavior, from reading and listening, from experimenting with personal leadership. After a while, each person's ethical system is at least a little different from anyone else's. (The disagreements we call politics; if they are violent, we call them revolutions.)

As in the evolution of law, precedent and precept are some help. An analysis of the exercise of public responsibility in some historical situation, where we now think we know most of the relevant facts, may aid in solving tomorrow's similar (but never identical) problems for ourselves; hence the heavy use of case method teaching in law schools, business schools, and schools of public affairs and administration.

Wise sayings from Mencius and Aristotle, the Bible and the Founding Fathers, not to mention our own parents, may likewise be useful but hardly controlling; with a little help from a concordance of the Bible or Bartlett's *Familiar Quotations*, it is all too easy to find some pseudo-scriptural basis for whatever one really wants to do. New principles do not need to be written, by the Public Executive or a ghostwriter; they all seem to have been uttered already by Old Testament prophets, Chinese and Indian sages, the ancient Greeks, and the teachers and saviors of the world's great religions.

These do not of course provide much guidance on what to do next—how to cope with riots and poverty and discrimination, whether to deploy a space-based defense system or build another office building, what to do and who should do it in Berkeley and Newark and Biafra and Vietnam. They are even less helpful in deciding how to chair a committee meeting or whether to hire Miss Smith. Some of our forefathers' wisdom may even be part of the problem. Pollution, urban decay, and the weapons of frightfulness are pretty directly traceable to the Age of Enlightenment.

Every ethically independent executive thus has to apply to immediate reality the notions about procedure gleaned from personal study and experience. But the most conspicuous component of that reality is the presence of other ethically independent individuals who are applying *their* differing criteria to the resulting behavior. This requires executives to develop judgments about the motivations of the publics in whose interests they presume to act, those same publics which will ultimately judge whether the executives measure up to a minimum standard of public responsibility for their time, place, and function.

In these circumstances a written code of ethics can never be comprehensive enough or subtle enough to be a satisfactory guide to personal behavior as a Public Executive. Louis Hector, a lawyer who served on the Civil Aeronautics Board, put it succinctly: general prescriptions, whether in the form of dos or don'ts, are bound to be "so general as to be useless or so specific as to be unworkable."

The "Will I Still Feel" Question

Lacking an affirmative code of ethics, I developed while I was working in the federal government a key question to ask myself just before getting committed to a line of action. The question was designed to reflect both the judgment that people-in-general might later make on my behavior and my own reaction in the face of that judgment. The question still seems to me well designed to compel me to project my own feelings in the dramatic rehearsal of imagined public scrutiny of my actions, and the procedures by which they are decided.

The question is not "Will I be criticized?" If I am operating in the area of public responsibility, the answer to that question is quite likely to be yes. The (to me) illuminating question is this:

"If this action is held up to public scrutiny, will I still feel that it is what I should have done, and how I should have done it?"

If those involved had asked themselves this question and answered it honestly, most of the famous instances of public corruption that enliven and debase our political history might never have happened.

Sometimes the issues are large—incestuous relations between the military services and their contractors, major diversions of public monies to private purposes. But the human drama and pathos don't emerge in the cases of intentional profiteering. They show up in ethically opaque behavior by upright people so confused by public complexity that the distinction between right and wrong gets blurred along with the line between public and private.

If General Harry Vaughan in the Truman White House had asked himself whether the transaction depended for its acceptability on its not becoming public, he would never have accepted the deep-freeze that helped defeat the Democrats in 1952. If Sherman Adams in the Eisenhower White House had not considered his relations with Bernard Goldfine an untouchable private affair, he surely would not have stained his image of New England rectitude by accepting the gift of a vicuña coat. When Bobby Baker, an assistant to Senate Majority Leader Lyndon B. Johnson in the 1950s, was trading senatorial influence for business opportunities, did he think his powerful sponsorship made him invisible? When Harold Talbott wrote endorsements for his private management firm, using his official stationery as Secretary of the Air Force, only the public outcry and his consequent dismissal seemed to illuminate for him the ethical issue involved. Supreme Court Justice Abe Fortas, whose reputation as a lawyer was built by purveying sound and sensitive advice to clients operating in the no-man's land of public-private enterprise, could not have banked a fee from a stock manipulator if he had asked himself the "will I still feel" question.

There have been efforts, notable more for courage than for practicality, to pass quantitative rules about the private relations of public servants. In Washington, for example, the issue of what gifts, if any, a government official should accept is a chronic source of private trouble and public entertainment.

Senator Paul Douglas of Illinois, an economist, tried to draw the line at gifts worth $2.50. "Some of my friends humorously suggest that this rule shows that I have little faith in my own ability to withstand temptation," Douglas said in a Harvard lecture. "They say apparently I can resist the allure of a $2.49 present, but not of one worth $2.51. I am willing to accept and indeed smile at these gibes. With all its borderline difficulties, the rule has helped keep me from major involvements and it has done so with a minimum of spiritual wear and tear."

Michael DiSalle, who became governor of Ohio, earlier headed the Office of Price Administration. He ordered employees of OPA not to accept as a gift anything that could not be consumed in twenty-four hours. I recall a stimulating evening when a group of young civil servants tried to apply this rule to the gifts our bosses were receiving. A Smithfield ham was clearly within bounds— though one man in the Bureau of Internal Revenue had testified to a congressional committee that he drew the line at a ham weighing twelve pounds. It was not so clear whether, if you had a large enough circle of thirsty friends, it would be within the DiSalle doctrine to accept a case of Scotch.

Perhaps the limiting case of ethical opacity was recorded shortly before Assistant Attorney General T. Lamar Caudle drew a jail sentence for corruption in a former job as United States District Attorney in North Carolina. Caudle, according to Senator Douglas, "testified that he used to leave the side window of his automobile open when he parked it, and that he was always surprised by the wide variety of presents that were generously and anonymously thrown into the back seat by unknown admirers and friends."

Some of Washington's most vivid illustrations of private confusions about public ethics occur at each change of administration, when those new presidential appointees who happen to be rich are pressed to sell their stock in private enterprises that do business with the government. The senators who interview the nominees do not really think a rich corporate executive is motivated by profit to take a government job. But someone who is going to manage public monies must not be seen to stand too close to the fuzzy line between public and private.

In January 1953, General Motors President Charles E. Wilson was nominated as Secretary of Defense. After two long days of public hearings in which Senators were urging the nominee to get rid of his very large GM stock holdings, Wilson made a revealing comment. "The thing that perhaps I overlooked myself," he mused, "was that not only did I have to operate honestly and fairly without prejudice, but all the people should also think that that was the way I was operating, and that part of it I did not quite appraise." The senators were stunned. How does a man get to be sixty-two years old and president of the world's largest corporation without having "quite appraised" the biblical admonition to avoid not only evil but the appearance of evil?

"If this action is held up to public scrutiny, will I still feel that it is what I should have done, and how I should have done it?" If a TV camera crew had been taking pictures at My Lai that day, would Lieutenant William Calley have killed those Vietnamese civilians huddled in the ditch? War diffuses the responsibility for life-and-death decisions, and the central ethical question left by Calley's trial—Calley was guilty of the murders, but who was *responsible?*—was never resolved. In part Calley has to be adjudged responsible. In the field, the local commander has considerable discretion.

The "will I still feel" question is intentionally two-edged. It is designed to prevent me (and anybody else who cares to use it) from playing God, taking the full ethical responsibility for a judgment which can ultimately be validated only by some relevant public. But it is also designed to avoid the equal and opposite danger: that an action about which I have doubts becomes all right if others—my colleagues in an organization, my professional peers, my family, my friends and neighbors—can be counted on not to object.

Judging your actions by what others would think is as risky as judging them by what you alone think. William Attwood reported in *Look* on "an extreme and ironic case of neo-moral conformity in Colorado, where a man who did not chisel on his income tax boasted that he did. To be well regarded by his friends, he pretended to be doing what he assumed the group considered smart." The case of young Charles Van Doren, who cheated to make a TV quiz program successful, was only an especially dramatic example of a person who thought he could transplant organizational ethics wholesale, without marrying them to a public responsibility concept of his own.

In another famous instance of the corruptive power of the mass media, Sam Snead found on the fourteenth hole of a televised golf tournament that he had one extra club in his bag and was therefore automatically disqualified. Instead of saying so forthwith, Snead finished out the match, but contrived to putt so badly that he lost. The show must go on, he must have felt. The National Broadcasting Company thought so too: in full knowledge of Snead's unusual way of disqualifying himself, the network later aired the match without warning the television audience that Snead had deliberately taken a dive during the last few holes.

People caught in ethical thickets such as these are often heard to blame their troubles on the System—the corruption of the mass media or the oppressive weight of the institution they serve. Thus a TV producer who is a little ashamed of assuming moral responsibility for loading the airwaves with half a dozen lurid stories a week will tell you that the public insists on it, or that the advertisers require it. But what makes a modern Public Executive free (even the military are only partly an exception) is precisely the ability to go and do something else. If someone does not go and do something else, the rest of us have the right to presume that any moral discomfort is offset by the more tangible comforts of the position. You cannot claim to be *both* ashamed *and* oppressed—for that would relieve you of the private responsibility for your public actions, which is, as Mark and Charles Van Doren seemed to agree, the very definition of integrity.

The Uses of Public Outrage

The first line of defense against anti-public actions by Public Executives is to develop their own moral sensitivities. The second line of defense is public outrage. Both grow best in the open.

The 1960s in America saw the greening of public outrage, combined with a growing insistence that decisions on public policy be more openly arrived at. The war in Vietnam was a particularly good subject for healthy indignation: not only did it clearly become a costly, inconclusive, and embarrassingly unilateral adventure, but the process by which President Johnson committed the nation and the Senate to major combat on the Asian mainland struck many people as stealthy.

During this same period students and many others, not all of them young, were experimenting with public outrage directed at many other targets—racial discrimination, police tactics, restraints on free speech, censorship of the press, poverty, the sluggishness of educational reform, the degradation of the environment, the invasion of privacy, antiballistic missile systems, incompetent judges, unsafe automobiles, sonic booms, price gouging, and urban sprawl and ugliness.

Much public outrage has taken the form of organized protest by petition, march, and mass visitation, shading over into sit-ins, forcible restraint (usually of Public Executives), vandalism, and violence. The most impressive new lifestyle in America of the 1960s was not the informality of dress, the public surfacing of sex, or the eighteenth-century hair length; it was the propensity of Americans to demonstrate in public when aroused. This had long been a natural mode of action for delegates to political conventions and students living in college dormitories. But since the sixties, the street rally and the mass visitation have been widely used by all kinds of people in every part of the political spectrum.

Yet the staying power of spontaneous citizen protest was not impressive. An especially outrageous public action (the unanticipated invasion of Cambodia, the premature use of police on campus) can trigger a vigorous, even violent reaction for a few hours or a few days; but the half-life of popular indignation is short. Citizen demonstrations are effective in stopping or delaying actions by Public Executives, but the sustained effort required to get something new started or (*a fortiori*) finished was generally beyond the capacity of citizen and student protest in the 1960s.

Staying power requires a wide consensus among the protesters on a minimum where-are-we-trying-to-go doctrine. The Communists did as well as they did in Europe and Asia because they organized in the service of what they claimed was an inevitable history. They had a Manifesto and a Book, and in Lenin and Mao Tse-tung they found brilliant tacticians who were good at adapting antique doctrines to fit the tactical requirements of the struggle for power.

The radical leadership of "the movement" during the 1960s lacked a doctrine to glue together the pluralistic energy unleashed by a variety of frustrations in a dozen cities and on a hundred campuses. Some protesters were not even sure they wanted to establish new institutions in place of the old, suspecting that human institutions as such are irremediable. But a revolutionary leader who distrusts organization and is allergic to power is unlikely to seize power or organize to hang onto it.

This skepticism of doctrine, combined with hostility to organized power, led some revolutionary leaders to be openly scornful of "causes." To generate some action, to shake things up, became for some an end in itself. On university campuses especially, the most militant leaders of mini-revolutions tended to narrow their substantive targets, and move as quickly as possible toward procedural issues to widen immediate support for action. They found that they could start with some substantive issue like ROTC or the Columbia University gymnasium or the right to use a "people's park," but to get a large excited crowd into the streets they had to shift the focus as rapidly as possible to a question of procedure—a failure of due process, "cops on campus," or whatever.

Analyzing the "events of May" 1968 at the Sorbonne in Paris, Raymond Aron described in a capsule the pattern of U.S. campus disruption: "teachers and students, divided among themselves on most subjects, find a factitious unity in opposing power and the police. If a few students want to bring on repressive measures by the civil authorities, nobody can prevent them from doing so. . . . This leads to the 'police brutality' which the doctrinaires of violence both desire and denounce."

If a substantive issue is useful only as a trigger, and is merely the tactical symbol of a System that is rotten to the core, the issue itself does not require careful research or the exhaustion of conventional remedies.

When the national Students for a Democratic Society selected the Reserve Officers Training Corps as a prime target on all American campuses, that was a signal that campus disruption, not a drastic reduction of the military influence in America, was their central purpose. On campus after campus the antiwar movement was lured away from the juiciest and most relevant targets—the national military-industrial complex, the size of the military budget, the continuation of the war in Vietnam—and concentrated instead on tweaking the local military toe called ROTC. The quality of the debate even on that subject was not high: ROTC was seen as a means to confrontation, not as a subject in itself. The confrontations were often achieved, but they left little residue. Meanwhile, the initiative on military spending, on the Defense Department's contractual arrangements, and even on troop withdrawal from Vietnam, was left with the Nixon administration.

Residue of Sixties Protests

On subjects other than war and peace, however, the spasm of protest in the sixties left behind the beginnings of some permanent machinery for mobilizing and aiming the public outrage.

Civil rights organizations grew out of racial protest, and remained to litigate in the courts and lobby in Congress and the state legislatures. Rioting in the cities left a strengthened Urban League and an Urban Coalition. Housewives' increasingly vocal objections to being cheated pushed the federal and some state governments into setting up consumer advocates, partly to do battle with the many other interests already encamped within the bureaucratic walls. Philanthropists gave money to organizations to help them improve the quality and targeting of outrage—though the fear of government regulation often constrained their courage. Legislatures, realizing they had delegated more than they intended of their real power to mayors and governors and presidents, brushed up on their right of inquiry, always a powerful instrument in mobilizing public outrage and enhancing their bargaining power with the executive branches of government.

The movement with the most charisma, and potentially the most staying power, was that associated with the name of Ralph Nader. A young law student gets interested in highway safety. He concludes that part of the trouble is the way the automakers build autos. He sets forth on a lonely crusade against General Motors. He writes a book, *Unsafe at Any Speed*, that catches the public fancy. General Motors collaborates by putting detectives on his trail.

He sues General Motors and collects a large sum, which he invests in establishing the Center for Responsive Law in Washington. Students and young lawyers flock to join or emulate him. And he finds he has created a new kind of institution, the public-interest law firm backed up by a public-interest research group, to do the homework required to keep the Public Executives in private corporations and government agencies aware of their public responsibilities.

Nader proved something of far-reaching importance—that it takes energy, brains, and careful research to keep Public Executives honest and alert, but it does not require vast resources or very large institutions. He himself would doubtless agree that this kind of monitoring service works best if its power, too, is diffused, uncentralized: a thousand Naders scattered around the country would be far more effective than a "Nader Organization" a thousand times the size of his relatively small and intentionally helter-skelter center.

The other public-outrage-mobilizing service that showed real signs of staying power was the environmental movement. Concern about the quality of air and water, the condition of the land and the degradation of the oceans, the mercury in the fish and the cyclamates in the artificial sugar, the phosphates in the detergents and the lead in the gasoline, the dangers of the colored dyes in our tissues and the chemicals in our bug sprays, and the general feeling that we were about to be overwhelmed by undisposable waste and unmanageable numbers of babies, grew so fast that some citizens in every community appointed themselves to cry havoc.

The volunteers were often not the most careful researchers or the most effective spokesmen. But in league with university scientists, disgruntled public servants, old conservationists, and young professionals bored with their normal career outlook but attracted by the burgeoning battles over ecology, they have enormously enhanced the public awareness of environmental dangers.

Role of the Media

Except in extreme cases, the executives in government agencies and large corporations and nonprofit agencies would not even hear about the public's present or prospective outrage if it were not reported, and in some instances generated, by newspapers, magazines, TV, and radio. If exposure is so important in preventing actions that are thoughtless of the public interest or deliberately designed to bypass it, the managers of communications media have a crucial role to play in this multilateral system of checks and balances. This means that the media managers, too, are Public Executives, and like others of their breed are responsible to no one or everyone. Who, then, checks these checkers?

Newspaper editors and TV-radio station managers are often heard in passionate defense of their freedom to publish according to their own lights, without prior restraint by the government's Public Executives. This freedom, like other freedoms enjoyed by large organizations affected with the public interest, is inherently constrained by the acceptability of its exercise to people-in-general.

During the moral crisis produced by Charles Van Doren's revelation that he was giving memorized answers to prearranged questions on national television, the network executives made their accountability explicit. "It is our responsibility," said NBC's Robert Kintner, "to make sure that these programs will be honestly conducted, so that the public can have confidence in all the programs it watches." Frank Stanton of CBS was on the same wavelength: "We are responsible for what appears on CBS. We accept that responsibility. . . . We are only obligated to do one thing and that is to be responsible to the American people."

The American people can no more leave the use of their airwaves to the unreviewed judgment of Public Executives in the networks than they can leave stream pollution to the unreviewed judgment of Public Executives in private industrial firms. A federal agency therefore licenses TV and radio transmissions—though this power has not been used effectively to deter cultural pollution of the airwaves. For newspapers, however, there is no comparable licensing service on behalf of people-in-general. If a barber wants to cut my hair, he has to have a license; if a newspaperman wants to cut my throat, all he needs is a word processor and some white space in tomorrow's edition.

The constitutional battle over the Pentagon Papers in 1971 emphasized how heavy and how unreviewed is the obligation of a newspaper's Public Executives to decide what they are going to print and when. The Attorney General was frustrated in three federal courts on the issue of "prior restraint" of the publication of Top Secret government documents, however procured. By their actions the courts, including the U.S. Supreme Court, said in effect that it is up to the editors to decide what is fit to print; the government can review that judgment after the fact but not before.

Case History: *The New York Times*

The judgment of editors is a sometime thing; consistency over time is hard enough for an individual, and harder yet for an institution whose personnel roster naturally changes.

In December 1962, *The New York Times* carried an editorial attacking the *Saturday Evening Post* for revealing actions of the National Security Council during the Cuban crisis six weeks before. The *Times* had itself voluntarily withheld information it had at the time, to avoid scooping President Kennedy on the announcement that Soviet missiles were present in Cuba. (The *Times* also knew more about Bay of Pigs planning, earlier in the game, than it revealed in its news columns.) In an editorial entitled "Breach of Security," the *Times*'s judgment on the *Saturday Evening Post*'s judgment was scornful: "How can advisers to the President be expected to give advice freely and easily and at all times honestly and with complete integrity if they have to worry about what their arguments will look like in print a few weeks hence?"

Eight and a half years and forty-five thousand American deaths later, *The New York Times* had concluded (in its decision to publish the Pentagon Papers on decision making about the war in Vietnam) that it was all right to publish Top Secret documents if a three-year period had elapsed between the confidential advice to the President and national publication by the *Times*. My own instinct favors the *Times*'s more recent interpretation of its public responsibility.

Perhaps it would sharpen the judgments and make the presidential advice more honest if all the advisers had to pass their advice through that piece of litmus paper: "How will I feel if this advice is later held up to public scrutiny?" Would all of LBJ's advisers have said just the same things in their memoranda if they had been asking themselves: "Do I want the American people to know that I was pushing escalation in the guise of tit-for-tat retaliation, at a moment when the president was beating Senator Barry Goldwater (his electoral opponent) about the ears for wanting to enlarge the war on the Asian mainland?"

The embattled Public Executives at *The New York Times* were more self-conscious about their own position than were some of their more uncritical supporters. "Who elected *The New York Times?*" somebody must have asked in the newsroom when the storm broke over the Pentagon Papers, because for several days the editorial page, James Reston's column, and Max Frankel's interpretative correspondence from Washington used that identical question as a foil for arguing that the *Times* was responsible to people-in-general, and was exercising that responsibility the best it knew how. The *Times's* passion about the war in Vietnam had prevailed over its earlier reasoning about the self-restraint of the press. As Reston had written in another connection two years before, "It is a time of strong passion and weak reason."

Who, then, guards the guardians? In the case of the newspapers especially, there is a strong case for a forum in which the Public Executives of the media have to sit down from time to time with the Public Executives from government, private business, universities, and other major structures of each community to face the uninhibited criticism of colleagues and justify the unreviewed decisions they make pursuant to their concept of what is good for people-in-general.

In Honolulu, the University of Hawaii took the initiative to set up the Community-Media Council to experiment with the idea that the quality of the public dialogue can be improved by getting some of the key Public Executives in town to meet once every three or four weeks with the editors of the two main newspapers and the four main television-radio channels.

In the absence of some such device, the situation is essentially unfair. The Public Executives in government are responsible to people-in-general through a legislature. The Public Executives in private enterprise are responsible to people-in-general through the communications media. The electronic media are in some sense responsible to the Federal Communications Commission. But newspapers and magazines are responsible in some sense to themselves.

How Open Is Possible?

If public ethics are in the hearts and minds of individual Public Executives, and if the ultimate court of appeal from their judgments is some surrogate for people-in-general, it follows that the procedure for making public policy decisions should be as open as possible. How open is possible—without destroying the basis for cooperation and community?

The value of openness is quickly established. Anybody watching the workings of government must be struck by the observation that the most controversial programs tend to be those that generate the least scandal and corruption. The reason is that a program constantly under fire, needing constantly to expose itself by replying to charges or defending its jurisdiction, is so revealed to public scrutiny that for its Public Executives honesty is not only the best policy but the only available option.

In Washington, it is no accident that matters that frequently get to the White House are so often better handled than those that do not. The housing programs of the federal government worked off in a corner by themselves for years, dealing directly with the housing industry and developing an intricate network of corruption that seemed to the Public Executives involved to be the natural order of things until Congress discovered large private profits being made at the public's expense.

The foreign aid program, on the other hand, spent more than $50 billion before scandal began to appear around the edges. In its first decade so many departments and agencies were fighting for the right to manage chunks of the foreign aid program that the program was the subject of monthly, sometimes even weekly, concern to the President, the Congress, the media, and the public. Only later, when the jurisdictional issues were settled and the aid program became, comparatively speaking, an old-line government agency, did the unnatural relations between its public and its private functions begin to develop.

We cannot arrange for every program affected with the public interest to be controversial so as to keep it honest. The alternative is to make sure that the main considerations that affect each decision, and the people mainly involved in making it, are exposed to the public in an understandable way.

Here too we face, as often in public affairs, a dilemma. It is easy to say that all decision making should be open to the general public. "Open covenants openly arrived at," said President Woodrow Wilson, but found that he could not follow his own rule and indeed consulted so little with Congress about his pet project, the League of Nations, that it failed to be ratified by the U.S. Senate.

Radical groups on campus have been verbally Wilsonian, proposing decision procedures that provide a vote for whoever comes to the meeting, and then making sure the meeting goes on for so long that most of the less passionate voters get hungry or sleepy and leave before the vote is taken. Open meetings of public boards and committees are also a perennial subject for editorial advocacy by the media. But every decision-making body develops some device for private discussion of differences among the people with the most responsibility.

In a newspaper office it does not occur to the editor to open up to the public, with cameras and microphones and all, the daily sessions in which the editorial-page staff argues out what will be presented as the newspaper's editorial opinion the following day. Similarly, in governing boards (of regents, trustees, or directors), in regulatory commissions, in regular government departments, or in corporate executive suites, there must always be provision for talking out in private the most controversial issues, for compromise and face-saving and graceful backing down. When boards are required by law to have all their meetings in public, that just increases the frequency of lunches and dinners among their members, as they negotiate in informal caucus the positions they are going to take in the formal meetings.

A realistic policy of openness starts with the Public Executives themselves. Every Public Executive—in a public or in a private agency—might well ask a self-question several times a day: "Does this action of mine really have to be taken behind a curtain?" If its validity *depends* on its secrecy, something is probably wrong with the picture.

At a minimum, the Public Executives and the legislative bodies from which they derive their authority and funds can arrange to discuss in public the major policy dilemmas with which the Public Executives are struggling from week to week. These cannot be kept secret anyway. They quickly become obvious to any reporter or citizen or public-interest lawyer who wants to probe behind the porous curtain of institutional privacy. Since the executives themselves have a stake in public understanding and consensus, they will often have an incentive to discuss with the affected publics the rationale for a move, and the alternative options considered and rejected, before rather than after a decision is taken.

Those "Odd American Notions"

Adolph Berle, the most philosophical member of President Franklin D. Roosevelt's "brains trust," once wrote (with obvious approval) about those "odd American notions that absolute power should not exist, that countervailing power ought to be maintained, and that legitimacy of any power must rest upon a popular base."

Early in the twentieth century, Berle didn't quite visualize a horizontal society, where nobody is in charge and therefore everybody has a chance to be partly in charge. But it is clear enough now that those "odd American notions" about countervailing power and plural initiative *can* work if three conditions can be met:

- More than a million Public Executives, in private and paraprivate and public organizations, develop their own personal definitions of the public interest.

- There exist enough independently organized ways of mobilizing the public outrage (the people who

do the organizing will also be Public Executives by
our definition).

- The processes of decision are open enough to permit
  representatives (including self-appointed representatives) of people-in-general to follow the play, recognize
  the players, and blow the whistle when they don't think
  the attitudes of the Public Executives are public enough.

A young professor named Woodrow Wilson recommended in
1887 that government administrators should "combine openness
and vigor . . . with ready docility to all serious, well-sustained public criticism." It is still good advice—but it now applies to all the
men and women who carry public responsibility, whether or not
they happen to be working for the government.

Commentary on Chapter Thirteen

Three years after I had left the University of Hawaii, I was invited to give the fourth annual David D. Henry Lecture at the University of Illinois. David Henry had been president at Illinois for sixteen years, 1955 to 1971, and was widely recognized as a successful and durable executive leader in American higher education. The sponsors said they hoped I would reflect on "what it was like to be a university president."

My experience had given me some starting clues. I had learned that university presidents are expected to know it all but keep their omniscience well hidden; to be responsible for whatever happens at their university, especially controversial public comments by faculty members or unpopular public behavior by students; but to be deferential to all the parties at interest—students, parents, professors, administrators, regents, legislators, the governor, numerous off-campus special interest groups, the media, and hundreds of federal and international visitors each month. That meant I had to try continuously to take everything and everybody into account. It was thus an interesting challenge to think of myself as "a situation-as-a-whole person."

This essay is partly based on my reflections for that 1977 lecture. That's why some of the examples come out of my five years of managing a state university with nine campuses and more than fifty thousand students. But what I'm pointing up here is a larger lesson: our future needs to develop more and more leaders who, no matter what they are doing in whatever field, come to feel broadly responsible for the much wider context in which what they are doing has to be done.

I'll say it again: In a system where nobody's in charge, everybody has a chance to be partly in charge. Most people will not, for one reason or another, be inclined to reach for that brass ring. But those who do will be wise to try thinking of themselves as situation-as-a-whole people.

13

The Situation-as-a-Whole Person

A Passion for Paradox

Louis Brownlow entitled the story of his executive life *A Passion for Anonymity*. I have managed to remain anonymous without really having a passion for it; if I were to unfold the story of my own executive experience, I would have to call it something like *A Passion for Paradox*. Truth does seem to come wrapped in paradoxical packages, as Lao-tzu already knew 2,500 years ago. ("The truth often sounds paradoxical," *Tao Te Ching*, #78.) The art of executive leadership is above all the leader's capacity to hold contradictory propositions comfortably in a mind that relishes complexity.

The central paradox of large-scale administration is all too clear. Many years ago Sir Isaiah Berlin (in one of his *Conversations with Henry Brandon*) described it in five incandescent sentences:

> As knowledge becomes more and more specialized, the fewer are the persons who know enough . . . about everything to be wholly in charge. . . . One of the paradoxical consequences is therefore the dependence of a large number of human beings upon a collection of ill-coordinated experts, each of whom sooner or later becomes oppressed and irritated by being unable to step out of his

box and survey the relationship of his particular activity to the whole. The coordinators always did move in the dark, but now they are aware of it. And the more honest and intelligent ones are rightly frightened by the fact that their responsibility increases in direct ratio to their ignorance of an ever-expanding field.

Once again, with feeling: your responsibility increases in direct ratio to your ignorance of an ever-expanding field. The most thoughtful voices among us keep returning to this theme. "If we are to retain any command at all over our own future," says John Gardner, "the ablest people we have in every field must give thought to the largest problems of the nation. They don't have to be in government to do so. But they do have to come out of the trenches of their own specialty and look at the whole battlefield."

Missing: Integrative Thought

Of course none of us is trained for the scary profession of managing more while knowing less. No university in the world yet offers a Ph.D. in "getting it all together."

When I managed a university system I noticed that we had many interdisciplinary courses listed in the catalogue. On inspection they mostly turned out to be "team-taught," that favored academic device for avoiding interdisciplinary thought. Team teaching too often means that three or four professors share the task of teaching the same group of students. What usually happens then is that each teacher teaches a separate discipline. It's the students who are expected to be interdisciplinary.

I complained about this one day in a gathering of deans, and could see their tolerant smiles at this presidential naïveté. "Don't take it so hard," said Terry Rogers, the irreverent dean of our medical school. "It's the same all over. In a modern urban hospital, the only generalist left is the patient."

What is normally lacking in university education, then, is an interdisciplinary role model up front by the blackboard. We all know that the only truly interdisciplinary instrument is not a committee of experts but the synoptic view from a single integrative mind. The history of chaos theory features unusually creative scholars with an unusual propensity to integrate knowledge across disciplinary frontiers. Yet the academic reward system often promotes those who remain close to their specialties and penalizes those who reach out to find connections with the rest of reality.

The Polynesians of Hawaii have a vivid image that describes the way incentives work in some academic departments. They speak of a large pail half full of crabs: when any one crab gets ambitious enough to climb out and see what the world is like outside the pail, the other crabs hook him back into the intimate society of mutual back-scratching below.

University students—who in my experience are often perceptive about what's missing in their own education—make the point by indirection. When they want to say something nice about a favorite teacher, they are heard to say, "Well, you know, like, he gets it all together."

The cafeteria of courses in a consumer-oriented curriculum simply doesn't place a premium on integrative thinking. But the real world increasingly requires people to think about an enormous range of interrelated fields in order to operate effectively in any one of them. So how will colleges and universities—built on the proliferation of valuable but narrow expertness—respond to the judgment of irrelevance laid on them by students and employers who vaguely sense a need for more integrative thought? That is still the great unreported crisis of American higher education.

The evidence of crisis conditions is no secret. More and more of the liveliest academic crabs are sidling out of the university environment, trading tenure for the chance to work in reward systems that encourage the ablest people to give thought to the largest problems.

A generation ago, in the 1970s, I tried to count the growing number of think tanks and found more than six hundred of them in the United States alone. I have lost count, but there are now thousands of such groups doing their intellectual thing under happily indecipherable banners such as research and development, technology assessment, operations research, survey research, cybernetics, policy studies, policy planning, systems analysis, strategic studies, integrative studies, urban studies, humanistic studies, public interest law, thought-leading-to-action, critical choices, conflict resolution, peace studies, environmental action, futures studies, and global perspectives.

In these new-fashioned enclaves, much useful research and integrative thinking goes on, and it contributes greatly to the quality of policy discourse. But the trouble with most of this wide-angle research and policy analysis is that the think tanks do not, and most of them cannot, do enough to educate new generations of able young people inclined to give thought to the largest problems.

That is and will remain predominantly the task of higher education. But it will have to be a new kind of higher education. As usual, the push for it will have to come from outside the academy, with the academic administrators (as usual) serving as the carriers of infectious innovation. This means that, as a prerequisite to the spread of holistic thinking among the products of American higher education, those who would be its leaders will have to be—or have the capacity to become—situation-as-a-whole people.

Always Our Turn

To be a situation-as-a-whole person is not a profession. It's an attitude toward all professions, a propensity to interest oneself especially in the interconnections among the traditional jurisdictions into which we have divided the life of the mind, a willingness to view every problem in global perspective, and one thing more—the presumption to feel personally responsible for the whole outcome of which any individual's efforts can only be a small part.

If we don't yet have a national energy policy, that may not be somebody else's fault. If something needs fixing, it's not necessarily someone else's turn to fix it. In a world where nobody's in charge, each of us who chooses the role of conscious coordinator has a special obligation: in some degree it's always our turn.

We don't yet know how to train situation-as-a-whole people; the evidence is that we are not yet doing it. But as a start it may help to note their distinguishing marks or features. They are the folks who seem to be interested in everything—and find that intellectual curiosity pays some very practical dividends. They are the people who, no matter what the subject, keep reaching for the wider view, looking to the longer time scale. And because they have come to terms with the emerging ethic of ecology, they are the public citizens best able to think and act in the widest perspective.

An Interest in Everything

It was more than four hundred years ago that François Rabelais set out to know everything that could then be known. Such an ambition in 2002, in the midst of the knowledge explosion, would be dismissed as mental illness. But it is still a healthy ambition to be *interested* in everything.

At least, I can testify from personal efforts that it pays to try. If you are going to practice being interested in everything, serving as a university president provides an almost daily occasion to learn something new—if you can avoid spending all your time on budget cutting and legislative relations.

At the University of Hawaii, one of my tasks was, of course, to bring the aloha of the university community to gatherings of specialized scholars and expert practitioners, in fields ranging from ocean engineering to Oriental philosophy. In accepting invitations to cut these intellectual ribbons, I routinely insisted that my aloha would include five or ten minutes of personal comment on the conference topic. I usually didn't know anything about the topic, so I had to read into some unfamiliar literature and interview the key faculty members involved, sometimes at considerable length.

In this manner, during a typical month, I could critique the turgid prose of philosopher Martin Heidegger; develop some instant prejudices about music education in the public schools; explain our floating city experiment to federal site visitors; describe the "Nixon shock" in Tokyo to a visiting convention of UPI editors; comment on the governance of Honolulu while introducing Mayor Lindsay of New York at the National League of Cities; and, in preparation for a conference on ancient Korean traditions, learn that the first ironclad warships in history were not the *Merrimac* and the *Monitor,* as American history texts would have us believe, but vessels designed by one Admiral Yi a couple of centuries earlier.

One dividend of this self-induced "continuing education" was a wide acquaintance with the university's best scholars in fields far removed from international politics, economic development, and public administration, my previous academic beats. Most of my new friends were professors who didn't normally find their way to my office—because they weren't generating procedurally difficult or politically embarrassing problems.

I even worked out an almost infallible method for evaluating members of a university faculty. I found that I was judging my faculty colleagues by whether, when I talked with them, I learned something from them. (They were doubtless judging me the same way.) It seemed probable that if a professor wasn't arousing my curiosity and stimulating my mind, that probably wasn't happening to the professor's students either. I don't suppose there is any way to patent this evaluation system, but it would certainly be less laborious than baking that three-layer procedural cake customarily in use for making university decisions about promotion and tenure.

Another dividend of this continuous exercise of intellectual curiosity, especially for administrators, is that it provides welcome

relief from the deadening effect on the human brain of constant preoccupation with the administrative process itself.

Anyone who helps govern a university soon learns the Gresham's
Law that procedure elbows substance off the leader's desk. It takes only
a little longer to realize that procedure is actually the surrogate for substance in education as in other fields. In five years as president of a university system, I do not recall that anyone—student leader, faculty
colleague, campus provost or chancellor, regent, legislator, or federal
visitor—ever disagreed with me explicitly on a matter of substance.
Of disagreements there were many. But the complaint would turn up
in camouflage: I had failed to follow the correct (that is, written) procedures, or I couldn't have been correct because there *were* no written
procedures; I didn't consult the relevant groups, or at least not soon
enough, or with their duly authorized representatives; I neglected
to prepare, in the proper form, a PPBS justification, a PERT chart,
a detailed schematic, a statement of budgetary implications, an environmental assessment, a certification of affirmative action; I omit-
ted to quantify the benefits, request the attorney general's opinion,
call a public hearing, or provide the requisite number of copies.

Such procedural objections, even trivial ones, can devastate a
plan of action. Especially in a large meeting, most of those present
are sufficiently inattentive, apathetic, confused, or hungry to favor
postponement by means that don't require hard thinking about the
substantive course of action being proposed.

Modern society has developed many highly effective ways of
retarding change and smothering innovation. Some of the most
effective have been grown in the hothouse politics of higher education where, as the old canard has it, the stakes are small and the
men of honor are often outnumbered by the men of principle. To
focus for twelve hours a day on untangling procedural snarls and
neglect to participate in the intellectual excitement that is
unleashed by your administrative action is to get mesmerized by the
misery and miss all the fun.

The Wider and Longer View

Isaiah Berlin's paradox, by which our responsibility increases in direct ratio to our ignorance of wider fields, is equally in evidence in global politics and administration.

The elements of world affairs are often discussed as though they were separable problems that will yield to separate solutions. But Elliott Richardson, who held more Cabinet posts than anyone in living memory, said it all in a lecture on interdependence in Philadelphia in 1976: "Once you see that the knee bone is connected to the thigh bone and the thigh bone is connected to the hip bone, you can no longer pretend that they are separate."

We have now begun to see that all the well-researched problems—nuclear weapons, arms sales, poverty, affluence, environmental impacts, manmade dangers, and resource constraints—are so exquisitely tangled together that action on any one of them requires thinking about all of them—that is, thinking about the whole predicament, the world *problématique*. And that kind of thinking is required of more than a million executive leaders of this pluralistic polity in a many-centered world.

Indeed, that kind of thinking is now required of multimillions of leaders around the world. "We Mexicans," says the poet Octavio Paz, "have always lived on the periphery of history. Now the center or nucleus of world society has disintegrated and everyone—including the European and the North American—is a peripheral being. We are living on the margin . . . because there is no longer any center. . . . World history has become everyone's task, and our own labyrinth is the labyrinth of all mankind."

It is probably no coincidence that world history became everyone's task just as the general public was discovering ecology, the science of mutual relations between organisms and their environment. In a luminous essay about the "vibes" cells give to each other, Lewis Thomas observes that in order to sustain life, "using one signal or another, each form of life announces its proximity to the others around it, setting limits on encroachment or spreading welcome to potential symbionts." The earth itself might be thought of as an "immense organism" where "chemical signals might serve the function of global hormones, keeping balance and symmetry in the operation of various interrelated working parts, informing tissues in the vegetation of the Alps about the state of eels in the Sargasso Sea, by long interminable relays of interconnected messages between all kinds of other creatures."

Every branch of the ecological sciences—including studies of the weather, the oceans, the atmosphere, the ozone layer, and the like—sends a supporting message: we had better respond to Nature's "global hormones" that give us signals of life or death. We interdepend or perish. Essentially, what we are beginning to perceive is an interlocking system of limits—not "limits to growth" but limits to thoughtlessness, unfairness, and conflict.

In one dimension, the rich-poor or North-South axis, an emerging ethic of fairness suggests limits to poverty (perhaps a minimum entitlement to human needs merely by being born into the human family); and also limits to the share that the most affluent person takes from a global pool of resources that is flexible but finite. (The principle is familiar, though the practice is uneven, in the progressive income tax.)

In other dimensions, an emerging ethic of prudence suggests socially determined limits to the damage people do to their physical surroundings (air and water pollution, stripping of the land, thinning of the ozone shield); the dangers inherent in people-managed processes (family planning decisions, nuclear power plants, chemical reactions, traffic accidents, weather modification, genetic engineering); the rate at which people use up nonrenewable resources (fossil fuels, hard minerals); and practices that affect the renewability of renewable resources (soil erosion, destruction of wildlife, overcropping of farmland, overcutting of forests, overfishing of lakes and oceans).

Still another dimension limits the scale of conflict about limits. Shortages and the desperation and rivalries they intensify will provoke acute conflicts. The arms available for use in these conflicts, which are not only the conventional and nuclear instruments of frightfulness but also economic and monetary and psychological and chemical and biological and meteorological weapons, are no longer in the hands of an oligopoly of so-called powers.

The nuclear technologies especially give everyone a common stake in limiting the extension of politics by military means. Factions and nations and regional or ideological blocs are going to have to bargain with each other to stay within all the other kinds of limits *without* the option of turning to the nuclear weaponeers as a last resort. Because that resort is too liable to be the last, détente can never mean relaxation. Détente is the continuation of tension by other means—means other than mutual suicide.

A Promising Prospect

The situation-as-a-whole people we need as leaders of our nobody-in-charge society will have one natural advantage: they will be Americans, or will have spent at least parts of their lives in America.

The past that is in Americans, whatever their origin, is a rich experience of trying, as Madison proposed, to govern communities, states, and a nation through mostly horizontal relationships. We started with the notion that freedom is the power to choose, and decided as we went along that the obverse equally applies: power is the freedom to choose.

The traditional kinds of leaders (the well-known government officials, business executives, and heads of large nongovernmental organizations) will not be ruling in traditional pyramidal ways. The spread of knowledge and the growing desire of literally millions of citizens to share in mapping their own destiny makes that close to a twenty-first century certainty. Maybe that was what Lao-tzu was intuiting when he said, two and a half millennia ago, that "ruling a big country is like cooking a small fish"—that is, too much handling will spoil it. With all his wisdom and foresight, Lao-tzu could not have imagined the size and complexity of a country like the United States—or modern China, for that matter. Too much handling *from the top* is what spoils political governance these days. Governance requires plenty of handling, but the burden and excitement of governing now has to be shared among literally millions of people from every heritage, every profession, every community, every race and color and creed in an increasingly, delightfully multicultural nation—"all mix up," as they say in Hawaii.

Can millions of Americans come to think of themselves as leaders, and therefore as situation-as-a-whole people? Can they handle their growing responsibilities despite their growing ignorance of the details of the expanding complexity for which they will be responsible? Can the ablest people in every field be induced, by education and experience, to give thought to the largest problems in the nation and the world? The prospect is preposterous enough to be promising.

It is not easy, but I have found it to be great fun to try and think hard about the situation as a whole while working hard at some small piece of the macroproblem of human cooperation. I never thought I got very close to understanding it all. But I tried to remember that the closer I could come to relating everything to everything else, the more nearly I would be matching the interrelatedness of the reality outside my mind—and thus gaining in the capacity to act relevantly in my corner of the larger complexity.

So don't let any of the experts who have helped produce the mindless discontinuities of the world *problématique* tell you that trying to focus on the situation as a whole is unscientific, or unprofessional, or unrealistic. As Sam Goldwyn is supposed to have said about one of his critics: "Don't pay any attention to him. Don't even ignore him."

Commentary on Chapter Fourteen

During most of the 1980s I was once again dean of a graduate school, the University of Minnesota's new Hubert H. Humphrey Institute of Public Affairs. One of the perquisites of that kind of job is that you are frequently invited to speak about education—what's wrong with it and why, how it could be improved.

The groups that invite you don't take account of your limitations: if you're billed as an educator, they want to know what you think about science (even if you're not a scientist) and elementary education (even if you've never been a schoolteacher).

But I had worried enough about the whole U.S. educational nonsystem to treat each of these engagements as a chance to learn what American students, parents, and academics were worrying about. I had also, during the seventies, spent a good deal of personal time and effort promoting "global perspectives in education."

In this essay I have tried to put into one frame three ideas about American education that I think will be crucial to our future in the new century. One is that, if the governance of a nobody-in-charge society will greatly increase the market for leaders, an important part of citizenship education has to be education for leadership. That means everyone will need a healthy exposure to "education for breadth." And, since we Americans will be living in a turbulent world we will have to understand and take into account, a global perspective will be indispensable in all our learnings.

14

Education for Citizen Leadership

The Drivewheel of Citizenship

When nobody can be in charge, and some self-selected subset of everybody is partly in charge, educating for leadership morphs into educating for citizenship. In the upside-down pyramid, where the people really do make the policy, leadership is continuous dialogue—not acts but interactions between those who lead and those who follow, the leaders and followers often being different mixes of citizens depending on what is up for decision.

The preparation of self-selected leaders is an important part of the puzzle. But the whole puzzle is much wider: it is how citizens at large learn to make policy on issues that affect their destiny.

Education is the drivewheel of citizenship in the informatized society. With information now America's (and the world's) dominant resource, the quality of life in our communities and our leadership in the world depend on how many of us get educated for the new knowledge environment—and how demanding, relevant, continuous, broad, and wise (not merely knowledgeable) that learning is.

We now have a system of postsecondary education to which some three-quarters of our high school graduates aspire; in the new knowledge environment of the twenty-first century, all young Americans will need, sooner or later, to expose themselves to higher learnings well beyond what's available in schools from kindergarten through high school.

Postsecondary education will obviously serve multiple purposes: education as an investment (for the poor), education as a consumer good (for the affluent), education as a device for avoiding decisions about what to do next (for the unattached, the uncertain, and the unemployed). But whatever the purpose of "going to college," the social contract in American higher education is clear enough: colleges and universities, and especially the public colleges and universities, are the egalitarian means for making an aristocracy of achievement acceptable in a democratic society.

It is now part of our democratic ethos that if we apply the merit principle to a large enough body of students with a fair enough representation of previously disadvantaged kinds of people, the resulting discrimination is permissible. This double ethic suits the students fine: they want an equal chance to go to college, but they also want a job when they get out.

Of course, no one is much good at forecasting the job market: the science of what people will be doing for a living is still the most primitive part of a still adolescent discipline.

The critics of higher education are judging by a simple standard: if a job isn't awaiting every student with newly acquired credentials, then the system of higher education isn't working the way it should. Most educators, by contrast, think their most important task is not to train for a meal ticket the week after graduation but to educate for fifty years of self-fulfillment: to help students develop a capacity for learning that will be a continuing asset and a joy for decades to come. Their egalitarian target is not an equal crack at a first job, it's an equal chance at a full life.

In this longer time-perspective, the attempt to quantify human resource requirements is bound to produce nonsense. In a society of increasing information-richness, the content of many, perhaps most, jobs a generation hence is unknowable today—just as the children of yesteryear were unable, through the ignorance of their parents and guidance counselors, to dream of being astronauts, nuclear physicists, ecologists, computer programmers, television repair techs, or managers of retrieval systems. (Indeed, not so long ago there wasn't such a job as "guidance counselor" in an American school system.) Already in 1975, the U.S. Department of Labor was guessing that by the year 2000, two-thirds of 1974's kindergarten students would be filling jobs that did not yet exist.

Work in the Knowledge Society

I have set down elsewhere my skepticism of efforts to foretell a certain future. Do not suspend your own skepticism as I now try, with an impressionist's broad brush, to project the kinds of work that are bound to be especially valued in the knowledge society of the future.

There will obviously be—there already is—much more information and services work, and proportionately fewer production jobs, to be had. Machines will keep on eating up the routine and repetitive tasks. The jobs left for people to do will require more and more brainwork—and more skill in people-to-people relations, which machines are no good at.

"Computer literacy" is already part of knowing how to read, write, compute, and communicate. (That doesn't mean more than a rudimentary understanding of the architecture and electronics of microprocessing. It does mean understanding what computers can do for us—just as most of us understand how to use household appliances without being able to repair them.)

Despite tenure systems and retirement benefits, people will move around even more than they do now—from place to place, from function to function, from career to career.

Work, and therefore education for work, will become less competitive and more organized around cooperation.

There will be a growing market for education as a nonpolluting leisure-time consumer good. Already some union contracts entitle workers to time off for education; the last time I looked, Italian metal workers had a contract right to 150 hours of education a year.

A growing proportion of the demand for higher education will be for recurring or lifelong education—now the international inwords for what used to be called adult or continuing education.

Education for leadership in varying forms will be a growth industry, because the proportion of the population that performs some leadership functions will keep growing. And leadership educators will increasingly explore such nonrational mysteries as "creative leadership," "intuitive leadership," and "spirituality and leadership."

More and more people will work at the management of international interdependence—in the federal government but also in state and city governments, in multinational corporations, private voluntary agencies, and international organizations both public and private (that increasingly fuzzy dividing line). International travel, for work and for leisure, and the expansion of global telecommunications will also keep spreading—and swelling the demand for people with a capacity for cross-cultural empathy.

This is a vision of full and fulfilling employment. Will there be enough jobs to go around? No one can know for sure. But what Harold Bowen was saying in the 1970s still seems a good guess in the first decade of the twenty-first century: that "two centuries of history have revealed no secular trend toward greater unemployment as technology advances." There is no finite amount of work to be divided up among a given number of workers. Work, along with capital, expands with our capacity to use what is new in new ways for new purposes.

What is less certain, as the complexity of everything grows, is the prospect for our capacity to educate a growing proportion of our population to aim our extraordinary talent for scientific discovery, our unexampled capacity to convert scientific insights into useful technologies, our bent toward doing what's never been done before. We'll need a rapidly growing cadre of get-it-all-together professionals, educated in integrative thinking, the path to wisdom.

The Students' Intuition

How are we doing at teaching wisdom?

The academy's students, and its outside critics too, notice that the vertical academic disciplines, built around clusters of related research methods, are not in themselves very helpful in solving problems. It's all too noticeably true: no real-world problem can be fitted into the jurisdiction of any single academic department. For example: As every urban resident knows, we know every specialized thing about the modern city—but we find it hard to "get it all together" so as to make the city livable, efficient, safe, and clean. In agriculture, by contrast, it was university-based science and its delivery to farms in every county that created the miracle of U.S. food production.

As they awaken to problem solving, college and university students gravitate to those of the academy's offerings that seem to promise an *interdisciplinary approach*. These offerings are sometimes disappointing. A course on environmental issues may be taught by an evangelist less eager to train analysts than to recruit zealots. A paid workshop on a so-called problem may mask a research contract for a client (a government, a corporation, a wealthy donor) who knows the answer and is looking for an academic seal of approval for a predetermined course of action.

Even so, many students prefer offerings that promise to cut across the vertical structures of method and help them construct homemade ways of thinking about the situation as a whole.

The revolt against methodology is also powered by the quickening interest in ethics, which started even before Watergate. A growing number of students come to college after some life experience—in the military or on a job or in a commune. They are groping for purpose, for effective ways of asking "Why?" and "Where are we supposed to be going anyway?" Disciplines that seem neutral about purpose, modes of analysis that are equally usable to kill people or build low-cost housing, make these students uncomfortable.

The students' intuition may not be wrong. Yet they face an impressive phalanx of opposition to their instinct that the vertical disciplines should be stirred together in problem-solving, purpose-related combinations. Access to academic journals, professional repute, and promotion and tenure are not achieved by having lunch with colleagues from other departments. And education's external critics for once agree with the academics: the division of knowledge into manageable compartments enabled the alumni to develop self-esteem and earn a decent living, so why does the curriculum have to be changeable, complicated, controversial?

But doesn't the new knowledge environment place a much greater premium on integrative thought? Won't we have to take a new look at educational systems that award the highest credentials for wisdom to those who master the narrowest slices of knowledge?

Wanted: Integrative Minds

We are born with naturally integrative minds. I suspect that a newborn baby knows from the start, by instinct, that everything is related to everything else. Before children are exposed to formal education, their curiosity is all-embracing. They haven't yet been told about the parts, so they are interested in the whole.

The more we learn, ironically, the less tied together is our learning. It's not situation-as-a-whole thinking, it's the separation of the specialized kinds of knowledge that (like racial prejudice) "has to be carefully taught."

The holistic learning comes especially in grades K to 4; the fourth-grade teacher is perhaps the premier generalist in our society. (Think of the variety of subjects on which a fourth grader is likely to ask the question "Why?") Further up the ladder of formal schooling, we do manage to persuade most children that the really important questions start with "When?" and "Where?" and "How?" and especially "How much?" Fortunately for the nation and the world, some young citizens persist in asking "Why?"

Jasmina Wellinghoff, a Twin Cities scientist and writer, wrote about her first grader:

> When my six-year-old learns that we heat the house with forced air, she immediately wants to know who is forcing the air, where natural gas comes from, and how it got stuck underground. After I have done my best to explain all this, comes the next question: "If we didn't

have natural gas, would we die in the winter?" There you have it. Geology, engineering, physics and biology, all together in a hierarchy of concepts and facts.

However, a few years from now my daughter will be studying the structure of the earth's crust, combustion, hydraulics, and the classification of living beings—all in different years and quarters, neatly separated, tested, and graded.

Everyone seems to know that out there in the real world, all the problems are interdisciplinary and all the solutions are interdepartmental, interprofessional, interdependent, and international.

Yet our institutions start with a heavy bias against breadth. It has been a useful bias: the secret of success of the Scientific Revolution was not breadth but specialized depth. Chopping up the study of physical reality into vertically sliced puzzles, each to be separately deciphered by a different analytical chain of reasoning (a *discipline*), made possible the division of specialization and of labor.

But one thing led to another, as E. B. White thought it would ("Have you ever considered how complicated things can get, what with one thing always leading to another?"). The resulting complexity now makes it imperative that these differing analytical systems be cross-related in interdisciplinary thinking and coordinated action. Those who would lead must therefore get used to thinking integratively.

The trouble is, our whole educational system is still geared more to categorizing and analyzing the patches of knowledge than to threading them together—even though it's the people who learn how to thread them together who will be the leaders of the next generation. What should we be helping them learn, for this purpose, during the years they are full-time learners?

It would be nice if the dilemmas were simple. But the ancient clashes between training and education, between vocational and general, between honing the mind and nourishing the soul still divide the outside critics, divide the professional educators, and divide the students too.

Just now our favorite way to resolve these dilemmas is to delegate them to the individual student. We "maximize the student's options" by creating a bewildering proliferation of courses and programs of study, a cafeteria of the intellect using what the food service experts call the "scramble system."

For the limited numbers of students who know just what they want and why, that kind of new freedom doesn't work badly. But most students need, and expect, some guidance in creating an intellectually nutritious trayful of reading, discussion, writing, computing, and work experience.

A New Kind of "Core"

My guess is that if U.S. schools and colleges continue to proliferate courses, external pressure groups and the state and federal governments will sooner or later impose social and economic and even political criteria for curriculum building. If our ultimate curricular principle is the cop-out called "maximum options," the outsiders will, in the end, tell the academics what to teach and the students what they can learn at the public's expense.

The answer, as usual, is not to settle the argument by choosing one of a dilemma's horns or the other. Honing the mind and nourishing the soul are both functional in the new knowledge environment. What we need now is a theory of general education that is clearly relevant to life and work in a context that is more and more based on the information resource—a rapidly changing scene in which uncertainty is the main planning factor.

Perhaps, in the alternating current of general and job-oriented education, it is time for a new synthesis, a new "core curriculum"—something very different from Columbia's World Civilization, Syracuse's Responsible Citizenship, or Chicago's Great Books, yet still a central idea about what every educated person should know, and have, and try to be.

Such a core is not going to have much to do with learning facts. It is said that each half hour produces enough new knowledge to fill a twenty-four-volume edition of the *Encyclopaedia Britannica*—and even when so much data can now be put on a single optical disk, that still makes it accessible only to those who already know what they are looking for. Most of the facts children learn in school are now unlikely to be true for as long as they can remember them.

The last time I took physics—in secondary school—I was told the atom couldn't be split. That information has not served me well in the nuclear era. When I got to graduate school and learned about Keynesian economics with a young Oxford tutor named Harold Wilson, I learned that inflation and recession were periodic but occurred at opposite ends of the business cycle; the idea that they might get glued together in persistent stagflation was not mentioned. This remembered learning wasn't very useful to me in the late decades of the twentieth century; it didn't seem to work very well for Prime Minister Harold Wilson, either.

What students need above all is the rechargeable batteries of general theory with which to energize their processing of the shifting "facts" they encounter in a lifetime of varied experience. If, however, we think hard about the requirements of the new knowledge environment and consult the instincts and perceptions of our own future-oriented students, I think we could construct a new "core curriculum" for American citizenship from such elements as these:

- Education in integrative brainwork—the capacity to synthesize for the solution of real-world problems the analytical methods and insights of conventional academic disciplines. (Exposure to basic science and mathematics, to elementary systems analysis, and to what a computer can and cannot do, are part, but only a part, of this education.)

- Education about social goals, public purposes, the costs and benefits of openness, and the ethics of citizenship— to enable each educated person to develop personal answers for two questions: Apart from the fact that I am expected to do this, is this what I would expect

> myself to do? and Does the validity of this action
> depend on its secrecy?

- A capacity for self-analysis—through the study of ethnic heritage, religion and philosophy, art and literature, the achievement of some fluency in answering the question, Who am I?

- Some practice in real-world negotiation, in the psychology of consultation and the nature of leadership in the knowledge environment.

- A global perspective and an attitude of personal responsibility for the general outcome—passports to citizenship in an interdependent world.

A Global Perspective

A word, in conclusion, about the last of these new imperatives. Education for an ecological worldview requires us all to stop pretending that there is a thick black line between domestic affairs and international affairs.

The blurring of the distinction between *domestic* and *foreign* was brought home to me in the early 1970s, when in Hawaii we took inventory of the state university's international relations and found 298 separate arrangements linking our academic community to foreign governments, universities, research institutes, and development projects. We concluded that the University of Hawaii was in fact an international institution—and every other large university was, too. It didn't seem to make sense to have a special office for international relations when those relations were so pervasive. The dean of international studies, we concluded, was the president of the university. Every course could, and should, be taught in global perspective.

This was *not* a plea for more academic attention to international relations, area studies, international economics, and diplomatic history. It was a much more far-reaching assertion: that *every* subject in the cornucopia of knowledge is better understood if the angle of vision is the ecological worldview.

The idea of "global perspectives in education" came of age in a hurry. In the early 1970s a few educational pioneers led by Clark Kerr organized around the idea that U.S. attitudes and policy about world affairs are the product of thinking by grown-up schoolchildren—so consciousness raising about America's interdependence had better start in our elementary and secondary schools.

In the late 1970s another contingent of pioneers, led by James Perkins, put back on higher education's agenda the central importance of foreign languages and international studies.

America's twentieth-century knowledge-driven revolution had started, after all, in its schools and colleges. A century of universal compulsory education had set us up for the U.S. economic miracle, a morality play in which the main actors were educated farmers, educated industrial workers, educated college graduates who went on to become prize-winning scientists and inventors, enterprising business managers, creative public executives.

So it would have to be in the schools and colleges, especially public but also private, where a global perspective, that priceless ingredient of strength and prosperity in America's future, would have to be nourished and promoted. The pioneers were clear they didn't want to abandon the basics. They wanted the three R's, now including higher-tech computation and communication, integrated with the learning of an American world view. Not "Back to Basics" but "Forward to Basics" was on their banner with the strange device.

Suddenly the device is not so strange any more. In the mid-1970s, "global perspectives in education" was a fringe movement at best; some even dubbed it radical, which it was in getting to the root of the matter. But a modern Rip Van Winkle, dozing for twenty years and awakening in the 1990s, would have been astonished to find this far-out idea somewhere near the mainstream in the sluggish flow of educational reform.

In May 1988, some fifteen hundred mostly paying customers from around the country gathered in St. Louis for An American Forum on Competitiveness and Educational Reform. They were teachers and administrators from schools and colleges and universities, and leaders in scholarship and business and politics, including five governors. I'm glad I was there. I learned something basic.

This was no in-group; to a surprising extent, even the prime networkers in global education, foreign language, and international studies didn't know half the people who had flocked to the newly popular banner. They came together to affirm, with some surprise at the suddenness of it, that they, who had thought themselves working in a thinly populated vineyard, were no longer the exceptions but were rapidly becoming the rule.

The story of our global interconnections was retold in St. Louis—familiar now, yet still stunning. Governor Richard Celeste of Ohio reminded us that it was Mahatma Gandhi who introduced Martin Luther King Jr. to Henry David Thoreau's essay "On Civil Disobedience." The young president of the American Stock Exchange, Ken Leibler, quoted an elder financial statesman, Paul Volcker: "You can't hedge against the world." During a coffee break, a scientist remarked to me on "the correlation between our scientific excellence and our permissive immigration policy."

And a paper by one of the world's authentic wise men, Soedjatmoko of Indonesia, compressed our complicated reality succinctly. The world economy, he said, is "anarchic, interdependent, and fragile."

Education for Wisdom

Most parents hardly know how to think about the tangle of cultures, currencies, and communities that is the world we are now so much a part of. But to our schoolchildren, such a complexity should be routine—if *we* remember to mention it to them in school, and college, and at that ultimate educational institution, the family dinner table.

Children and young students are not shocked to learn that everything is related to everything else, that their destiny is somehow mixed up with the fate of the other six billion people (so far) with whom they share a vulnerable planet. It's only later in life, after they have been taught about the world in vertical slices of knowledge, by different experts in separate buildings in unrelated courses of study, that they lose track of how it all fits together.

That's why children ask more Why? questions than anybody. It's quite possible for even young children to learn to think in systems. They live with interdependence every day—in families and home rooms and the local public park, which is a very complex ecological system. The ambience of mutual dependence, the ambiguities of personal relations, the conflicting ambitions of groups, are the stuff of socialization from our earliest years.

Once we learn that family and school and local government can be unfair, we are more ready to reckon with the global fairness revolution, the push for the satisfaction of basic human needs worldwide.

Once we know how to think about value questions in our everyday life and work (questions to which the answer is very often, "It all depends"), we are more than halfway to coping with value choices in that complexity of planetary puzzles called climate change, food production, energy use, population planning, development strategy, environmental protection, ocean law, trade, investment, and money.

Once, in short, the child can follow cause and effect around the corner, the child grown up should be able to follow cause and effect around the world. And with that kind of education for wisdom, the children who become leaders can tackle with less diffidence the Cheshire Cat's first question: "Where do you want to get to?"

"Global perspectives in education" is no longer an exotic idea in American education. It's more like the key to living and working in a world of diverse cultures, flexible systems, and competitive cooperation. We have to hope that we the parents and teachers of America are learning the lesson—so the next generations will be ready to take the test.

Commentary on "Aphorisms from Experience"

These notes, from experience in international diplomacy, were prepared as an op-ed article published as "Aphorisms for Diplomats" in *The New York Times* in 1983. You will have found versions of most of them in the essays in this book—for, I came to realize, they were really lessons from trial and error in trying to take the lead in a variety of contexts.

Afterword: Aphorisms from Experience

Each year, in each century, the management of conflict and cooperation seems to be near the center of the human experiment. Not long ago I sat down for a weekend and tried to figure out what I have learned during four decades about peacekeeping and peacemaking. The result: thirteen aphorisms from experience.

- No conflict, negotiation, settlement, or bargain is merely two-sided. For one week at the State Department, I counted the active sides of every issue that came across my desk. The number of sides was 5.3—which proves only that you can quantify any intuition if you try. If you don't get all the "sides" involved in the solution, they become part of the problem.

- A third party (it's really a sixth or seventh) is usually indispensable and often lacking. Conflict resolution requires some source of independent elucidation of the issues.

- Courage is directly proportional to distance from the problem. Near neighbors have too many axes to grind. That's why, in the early 1960s, the United Nations' best peacekeeping troops in the Congo were Indian, Malaysian, and Scandinavian. It is also why, in the seventies, the Organization for African Unity could not bring itself to deal with Uganda's Idi Amin.

- Force by itself is not power. Military muscle-flexing, as the Chinese would say, can merely be Big Noise on Stairs Nobody Coming Down. In international politics, for example, energy, money, trade, culture, data flows, and democratic values are all forms of power.

- Creep up carefully on the use of force. Violence is easy to escalate, hard to deescalate. It should never be used just to provide a release for the user's frustration. (A veteran Japanese diplomat once gave me some good advice: "Never get angry except on purpose.")

- Widen the community of the concerned. Problems and their solutions are multilateral. In such a world, unilateral both looks bad and works badly. The U.S. response in Korea in 1950 looked good and worked tolerably well because it was folded into a U.N. operation. The U.S. response in Vietnam in the sixties goes down in history as a unilateral failure, even though we had more foreign troops associated with us in Vietnam than in Korea.

- Voting is an inferior means of conflict management; consensus procedure usually works better. Voting takes a snapshot of a disagreement but often does not modify the behavior of the minority, who prefer their own rights to the majority's righteousness. The major breakthroughs in global cooperation (the Law of the Sea Treaty, the outer space treaties, the weather forecasting system, the triumphs in public health) have been accomplished by consensus procedure.

- Consensus is not the same as unanimous consent. Consensus means moving by "no objection" procedure: the acquiescence of those who care about the decision, protected by the apathy of those who don't.

- Process is the surrogate for substance. People will often clothe their substantive disagreements in procedural raiment: "Have you asked for a legal opinion?" "I didn't get a copy of your paper." "It's time for lunch." *Robert's Rules of Order* is often a bible for those who want to prevent action.

- Openness has costs as well as benefits. The central dilemma of participatory process is clear enough: How do you get everybody in on the act and still get some action? But everybody doesn't have to be in on everything. The world's work gets done by consortia of the concerned, coalitions of the willing.

- Our standards are not the world's standards. A viable purpose for American foreign policy is "to make the world safe for diversity"—the words of President John F. Kennedy heard round the world, sometimes forgotten in the actions of his successors. That policy won't work if—in Clarence Darrow's phrase—we judge others by their actions and ourselves by our intentions.

- People can agree on next steps to take together if they carefully avoid trying to agree on *why* they are agreeing. We would never have gotten an arms control agreement with the Soviet Union or a working NATO system or rules about the exchange of weather data and the use of the frequency spectrum if we had had first to agree on ideology. In international relations it's not management by objectives; it's management in spite of multiple objectives.

- Resolving conflict isn't always a Good Thing. Some tensions are promising: the global urge for fairness, insistence on human rights, competitive hustling, rising expectations. The problem is not just to keep the peace; it is to keep change peaceful.

Commentary on "The Whole Chessboard"

On September 1, 1981, in company with Bertrand de Jouvenel of France, I received the *Prix de Talloires,* a prize for "accomplished generalists" awarded by a Switzerland-based international club called Le Groupe de Talloires. The ceremony was held in a Benedictine monastery in Talloires, a village on Lake Annecy in southeastern France. That particular monastery was said to have been the source of more Christian saints—including St. Germain and St. Bernard—than any other. I had been asked to speak on leadership; my opening remarks, reproduced here, focused on what I later came to call the get-it-all-together profession. After that, I went on to spin out some philosophy of leadership—early drafts of what you've been reading in this book.

Afterword: The Whole Chessboard

In accepting the *Prix de Talloires*, especially in a monastery with such impressively saintly credentials, I do not hold with Christopher Fry in the matter of haloes. It was in *The Lady's Not for Burning*, I believe, that he wrote, "What, after all, is a halo? It's only one more thing to keep clean." I will try to keep your halo clean, to be sure. I will treasure it, too, because it's one-of-a-kind.

My delight in the Prize is its uniqueness. Every other international prize is for being an expert. The *Prix de Talloires* is for being a generalist, for bringing the experts and their expertise together in an effort to make sense, to make progress, to make the whole more valuable than the sum of its parts. Every other prize seems to be for chopping knowledge into pieces—the more unprecedentedly small the piece, the greater the reward to the first person to chop it off. The *Prix de Talloires* is, I take it, for trying to knit together the separate insights and diverse disciplines by which we have organized the life of the mind.

Breadth is the indispensable quality of leadership, but no successful leader makes the mistake of thinking that breadth is the antonym of depth. Everything really *is* related to everything else, and the person who plumbs the depths of his or her own specialty finds more and more connections with every other specialty. The astronomers who reach back in time to a big bang must, in scholarly honesty, ask the humanistic next questions: Why? and Who did it? and What does it mean? And so they come by the circuitous route of pure reason to conclusions that can only be acts of faith.

In similar fashion a person who is willing without embarrassment to be styled "generalist" is constantly impressed with the importance of *somebody* getting to the bottom of specialized questions. The leader-as-manager, indeed, is likely to be very unsuccessful unless—because he has once been an expert himself—he is good at judging whether the experts who stream through his office and create his information entropy are getting to the bottom of *their* subjects.

So, in celebrating the good judgment of the Groupe de Talloires in establishing a prize for generalists—I will not presume to judge their selection process, only marvel that they found this needle in their haystack—it is, I think, important for us *not* to imply that specialization and discipline and expertise are passé, obsolescent. A world of coordinators would be as much of a mess as a world of specialists. The need is to stir them together in the stew of social theory and action—which means that both these kinds of actors on the stage of society have to learn to live with each other, in a symbiosis of mutual respect born of mutual dependency.

But in that mutual relationship the leading edge, the front line of attack on the world's problems, has to be those whose function it is to say where to go, and when, and why. It is therefore of leaders that I will speak today, their function as innovators and their *formation*—in the French meaning of that word—as educated men and women. My central theme will surely be congenial to Le Groupe de Talloires. It is that the practice of leadership requires what Alfred North Whitehead called "that appreciation of the structure of ideas" which requires an "eye for the whole chessboard, the bearing of one set of ideas upon another."

Index